The McGinnis Journey through Ireland to America

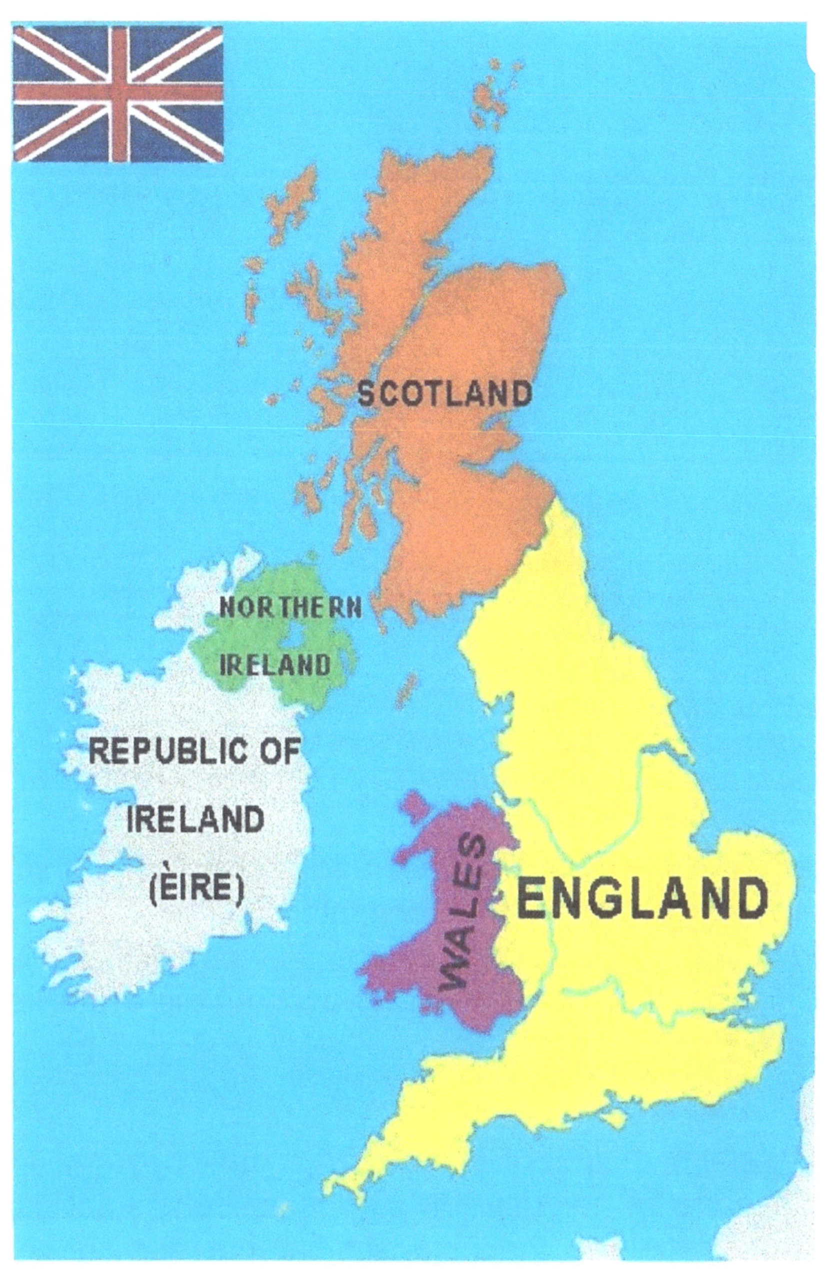

300 Years of Family History

One McGinnis Family History

(Compiled by Marti Bennett 2017-18...with research help from Brooke Drake)

This book is an attempt to follow your McGinnis trail, starting with James McGinnis. Emigrating from Ireland in the mid-1740's, your trail fans out to Virginia, and eventually to the western Pennsylvania counties of Clarion and Venango. The spelling of the surname McGinnis is uniquely American, more specifically Pennsylvanian. James and his ancestors spelled McGinnis differently, as you will see in following pages. The changing of name spelling is by no means limited to your line...and makes genealogy research more challenging!

As with many other people living in western PA, we share Irish diaspora heritage. The Government of Ireland defines the Irish diaspora as "all persons of Irish nationality, who habitually reside outside of the island of Ireland". This book is dedicated to Brooke, Heidi, and Alexa Drake...my 6th cousins on this line.

The most recent McGinnis in this line– Mary Ann McGinnis (1915-1974)
Picture taken about 1937

The McGinnis armorial shield shows a yellow lion on a green field with the red hand of Ulster on top. The arms illustrated are those of the ancient lords of Iveagh and reflect their rule in Ulster, incorporating both the red hand of the province and the principal heraldic symbol of royal power, the lion rampant. Family names, or surnames, as we use them, were unknown until the eleventh century. Before then, the Irish society consisted of an collection of tribes or clans. Individual members of the tribe were designated by a name indicative of some distinguishing personal characteristic. The origins of the McGinnis name come from the native Gaelic name, Mag Aonghusa. The Gaelic prefix 'mac' (frequently written as 'mag' before a vowel) indicates 'son of'. The word Aongus, or Aeneas, derived from aon, meaning excellent, and gus, meaning strength, and was Anglicized into various forms such as Aenus, Ennis, and Innis. The son of Ennis, therefore, became MagEnnis or MacEnnis. The family of McGinnis then is one of the oldest in Ireland. Through the years, Magennises have served in the House of Lords, House of Commons, and in ambassadorial positions. The present Lord Iveagh, is not directly related, but is of a related family. He heads the largest brewery concern in the world, *Guinness of Dublin*. Those bearing the surname in its various forms of spelling, including MacGenis, MaGennis, Guin(n)ess etc., are very numerous in the United States today, the greatest number, perhaps, being found in Pennsylvania. Philadelphia, it seems, was the point to which the early immigrants directed their steps, and from there they gradually spread to the interior and western part of the state, as well as to other states.

Voit DNA Results
(50% McGinnis 50% Voit Genes)

REGION APPROXIMATE AMOUNT

Europe 97%

Great Britain 52%
Europe West 23%
Ireland 11%
Scandinavia 6%
European Jewish 3%
Italy/Greece <1%
Finland/Northwest Russia >1%

West Asia 3%"Caucasus"What is Caucasus??? Primarily located in present-day: **Armenia, Azerbaijan, Georgia, Iran, Iraq, Syria, Turkey, Turkmenistan** .Also found in: **Bulgaria, Jordan, Greece, Italy, Kuwait, Palestine, Romania.**

When Roland B. McGinnis was born on 12 February 1879, his father, Charles, was 26 and his mother, Mary, was 19. He married Effie Erletta Rugh on 6 February 1907 in Lamartine. They had six children during their marriage. He died on 11 February 1946 in Oil City, Pennsylvania at the age of 66 and is buried in Lamartine, PA.

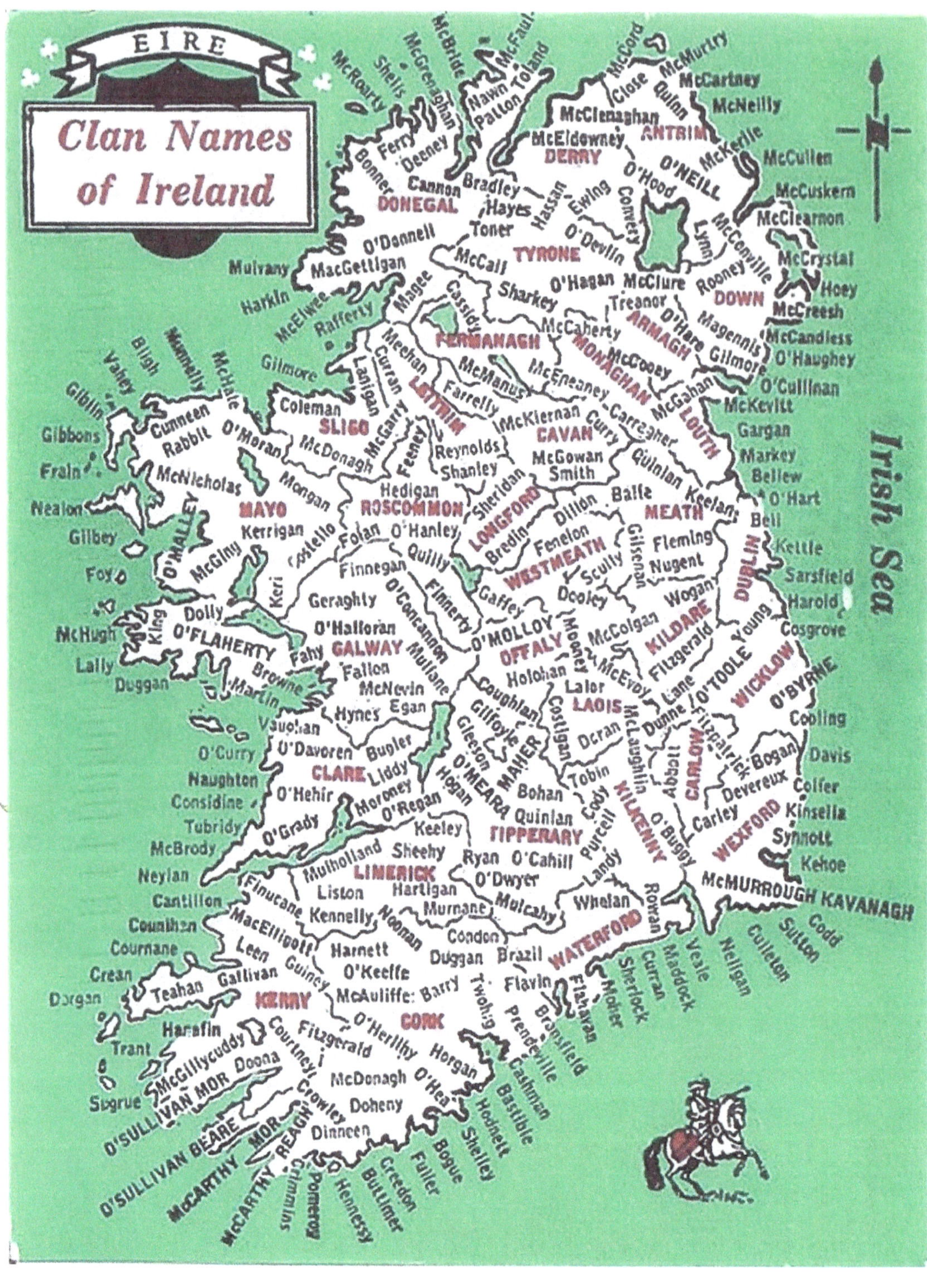

EIRE
Clan Names of Ireland
Irish Sea

DONEGAL
DERRY
ANTRIM
TYRONE
FERMANAGH
ARMAGH
MONAGHAN
DOWN
LOUTH
LEITRIM
SLIGO
CAVAN
MAYO
ROSCOMMON
LONGFORD
MEATH
WESTMEATH
DUBLIN
GALWAY
OFFALY
KILDARE
O'MOLLY
CLARE
LAOIS
WICKLOW
O'BYRNE
MAHER
O'TOOLE
CARLOW
O'MEARA
KILKENNY
WEXFORD
TIPPERARY
LIMERICK
WATERFORD
McMURROUGH KAVANAGH
KERRY
CORK
O'SULLIVAN BEARE
O'SULLIVAN MOR
McCARTHY MOR
McCARTHY REAGH

McFaul
McBride
Nawn
Patton Toland
McCord
McMurtry
Close Quion
McCartney
McNeilly
McRoarty
McGrenaghan
McClenaghan
McEldowney
McKettle
McCullen
Shells
Ferry
Deeney
Bonner
Cannon
Bradley
Hayes
O'Hood
Convey
O'NEILL
McCuskern
McConville
McClearnon
McCrystal
Hoey
McCreesh
McCandless
O'Haughey
O'Cullinan
McKevitt
Gargan
Markey
Bellew
O'Hart
Bell
Kettle
Sarsfield
Harold
Cosgrove
Mulvany
MacGettigan
O'Donnell
McCall
Sharkey
O'Hagan
McClure
Rooney
Treanor
O'Hare
Magennis
Gilmore
Harkin
McElwee
Rafferty
Magee
Cassidy
Meehan
Curran
Lanigan
McGarry
McManus
Farrelly
McKiernan
Curry
Carregher
McGahan
McEneaney
McCooey
Bligh
Vahey
Mannelly
McHale
Gilmore
Coleman
McDonagh
Feeney
Reynolds
Shanley
McGowan
Smith
Quinlan
Keelan
Giblin
Gibbons
Cunneen
Rabbit
O'Moran
Mongan
Hedigan
Sheridan
Dillon
Balfe
Fraln
McNicholas
Costello
O'Hanley
Quilly
Bredin
Fenelon
Gilsenan
Fleming
Nugent
Nealon
Gilbey
Kerrigan
Folan
Finnegan
Geraghty
O'Concannon
Finnerty
Gaffey
Scully
Dooley
Wogan
Foyd
McGiny
Keri
O'Halloran
Fahy
Mullane
Mooney
McColgan
Fitzgerald
Young
McHugh
King
Dolly
Browne
Fallon
McNevin
Holohan
McEvoy
Lane
Dunne
Lally
Martin
Hynes
Egan
Coughlan
Lalor
McLaughlin
Abbott
Fitzpatrick
Bogan
Davis
Duggan
Vaughan
U'Davoren
Bugler
Gilfoyle
Gleeson
Costigan
O'Buggy
Carley
Colfer
O'Curry
Liddy
Moroney
Doran
Tobin
Cody
Purcell
Devereux
Kinsella
Naughton
O'Hehir
O'Regan
Bohan
Quinlan
Landy
Synnott
Considine
Hogan
Keeley
Ryan
O'Cahill
Rowan
Kehoe
Tubridy
O'Grady
Sheehy
O'Dwyer
Whelan
Codd
McBrody
Mulholland
Mulcahy
Sutton
Neylan
Finucane
Liston
Hartigan
Murnane
Veale
Culleton
Cantillon
Kennelly
Noonan
Condon
Maddock
Neligan
Counihan
MacElligott
Leen
Guiney
Duggan
Brazil
Curran
Sherlock
Cournane
Harnett
Flavin
Maher
Crean
Teahan
Gallivan
O'Keefe
Flahavan
Dorgan
Harafin
McAuliffe
Barry
Twohig
Brassfield
Trant
Fitzgerald
O'Herlihy
Horgan
Prendeville
Cashman
Sugrue
McGillycuddy
Doona
Courtney
McDonagh
O'Hea
Bastible
Crowley
Doheny
Hodnett
Dinneen
Bogue
Shelley
Pomeroy
Crimmins
Creedon
Bullimer
Fuller
Hennessy

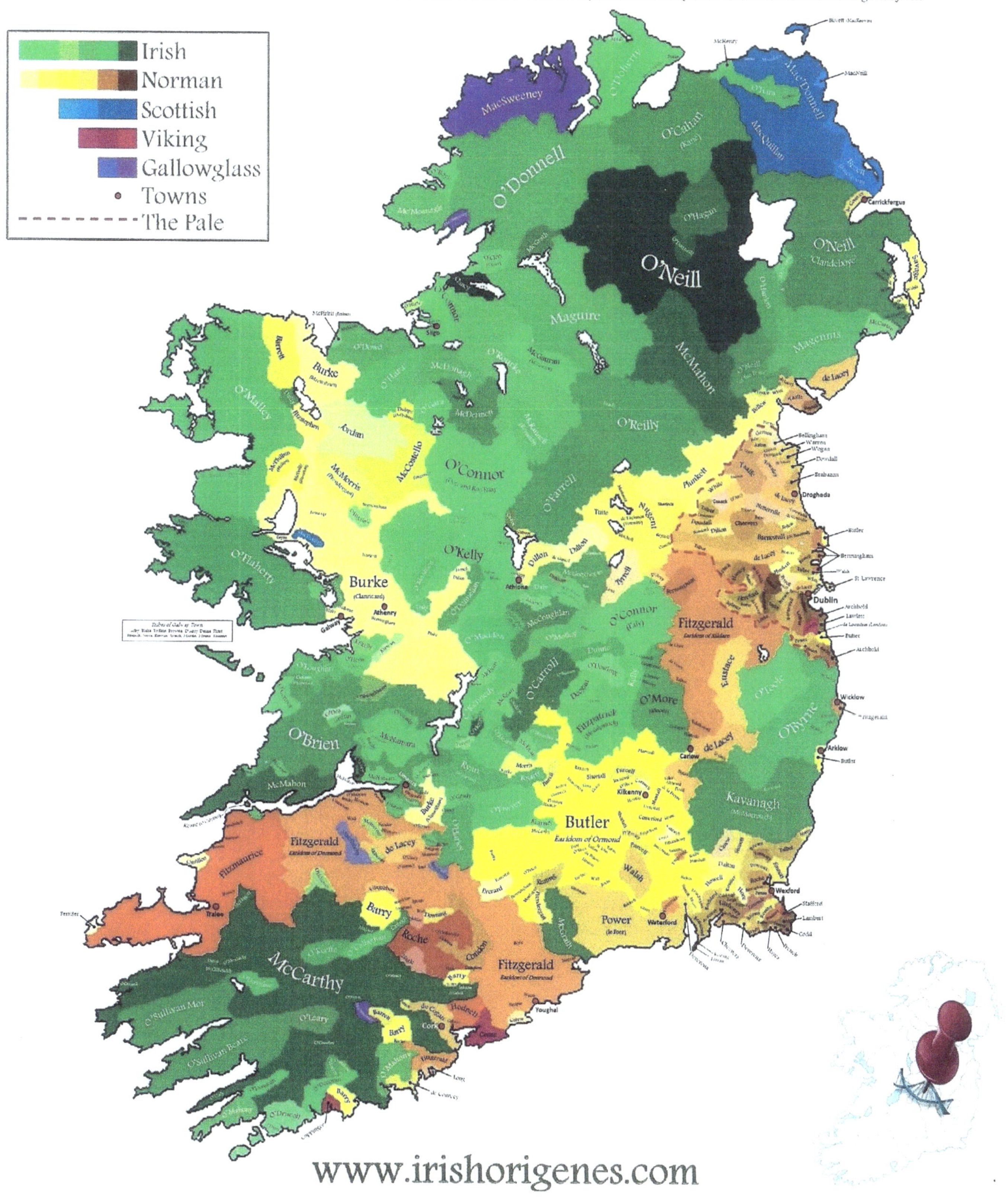

www.irishorigenes.com

The shield itself features an inverted St Andrew's Cross defaced with the arms of the Province of Ulster. The supporters come from both the former Scottish and Northern Ireland coats of arms. The Unicorn symbolizing the ancient Kingdom of Scotland and the Elk the historic Kingdom of Ireland. They both carry the flag of their respective kingdom and bear the arms of it. The base has stones from the Giant's Causeway (a symbol of civic Ulster pride) as well as the Shamrock (of Ireland) and the Thistle (of Scotland). The crest based on the Scots-Irish-American flag has an eagle supporting six stars in a saltire (A *saltire*, also called Saint Andrew's Cross, is a heraldic symbol in the form of a diagonal cross, like the shape of the letter X in Roman type.) again represent the significant contribution of the Ulster-Scots to the USA.

The motto is Scots for "Born Fighting" which is taken from the title of a book by US Senator James Webb, himself of Ulster descent, who wrote a history of the Scots-Irish from Roman times to modern day America. It reflects the often turbulent history and recognizes that often the main contribution of the Ulster-Scots in world wide British Colonies and the nations, that came after them, was a military one.

Who Do You Think You Are
Connections to Your McGinnis Ancestry and Scots Irish Heritage

The McGinnis legend begins thousands of years ago with an expeditionary force of 160 ships from what is now Corunna in northern Spain. About 450 BC, the eight sons of King Milesius and Queen Scotia invaded what is now Ireland. While landing in a storm which dispersed the fleet, five of the sons drowned. However, the remaining force, led by the three remaining sons, managed to route the natives, naming the island Ireland. That section of northern Ireland was called Ultonia, now known as Ulster.

Before Ireland's final conquest by England in the 17th century, the McGinnis and O'Neill clans were the main powers in Ulster. The McGinnis clan defeated English forces in 1380 and 1418, but the English defeated them in 1396, 1400, 1420, 1424, and 1453. The castle at Iveagh, County Down, is the traditional family seat.

According to an article written by Sean McGinnis in 2005: "In the 16th century, the McGinnis chiefs were often in conflict with Catholic authorities, and many became Protestants." This may help clear up the confusion as to whether the early McGinnis' were Catholic or Protestant. Some even went back and forth between the two religions. Donell Oge MacGuinness, born 1480 in Iveagh, Ireland, offers testimony to the theory the McGinness' were originally from Ireland, rather than Scotland. By the time of the Cromwell Revolution in 1641-1653, the family heads enthusiastically served the Royalist cause against the Puritans, and thus lost much of their land. This land was then planted with English (not the usual Scottish) settlers.

Throughout the 17th century, the McGinnis family consistently opposed the English, supporting the efforts of James II to regain the throne. However, after the conclusive English victory at the battle of Boyne in 1690, the McGinnis clan finally lost their vast hereditary lands in County Down.

In looking through the family tree, it becomes apparent that the later McGinnis' intermarried with another group of Protestant immigrants, known as the Scots-Irish. Many of us in western Pennsylvania have roots that link us to this group of historical immigrants. The Sloan line, which is the link between your McGinnis line and my Bell line, is distinctly Scots-Irish. The term Scots-Irish is actually a relatively new term, coined by Americans, for Ulster Scots or Ulster-Scots people. Prior to the Nine Years War of the 1590's, Ulster was the most Gaelic part of Ireland. It was also the only province that was completely outside English control. The beginning of the Scots-Irish story began in 1603, when King James V1, the Scottish Stuart king, became James 1, King of England, uniting those two crowns. He also gained possession of the Kingdom of Ireland, which at that time, was an English Crown possession. One of his first acts attempted to rein in the unruly Catholics in Ireland by seizing lands in northern Ireland and granting these seized lands to Protestant Scottish landlords and English merchants. Those recipients of estates were to then persuade tenants to migrate to the northern Irish province and take up farms. Those in Scotland, who accepted the invitation, became the ancestors of all the Scots-Irish in America. The Scots who went across the Channel to northern Ireland to participate in the "Plantation of Ulster" from 1610 onward, went to look for a better life, to escape miserable conditions, or simply for sheer excitement. The Scotland, from which the exodus began in 1610, was one of the poorest and most backward of European countries. Poverty-stricken, generally lawless, still lingering in the Middle Ages in the seventeenth century (and even into the eighteenth), with agricultural methods hardly better than primitive, there was every reason why an ambitious Scot should look elsewhere for improvement of his condition. The Scots-Irish story is one of progress from something near barbarism in 1600 to civilization, from ignorance to a passion for education, from backwardness in most fields to daring achievement, from static traditionalism to dynamic individualism – and all of this in the span of two centuries.

The Catholic landowners in the seized northern lands of Ireland were obviously none too pleased by the King's decision, which generally made life for the new and original settlers miserable, if not down-right dangerous. The attempt to dilute the Irish population by mixing religions, was adding fuel to an all-ready simmering fire. I found plenty of references to MagAonghusa family members engaging in battles in the 1600's, in support of the Gaelic Army, against the English. The city of Londonderry, one of the largest in Ulster, was a hot bed of military conflicts. On my recent trip to Ulster, I learned that Derry and Londonderry actually refer to the city of Derry. The Protestant section of town was called Londonderry, while the much larger Gaelic section was called Derry.

The McGinnis line seems to be from this area. One, Sir Hugh MagAonghusa, was noted in several Ancestry references, as leading successful battles where he defended his people's lands...and was later murdered by the same people whose lands he helped to defend. While northern Ireland today is a much safer area, occasional turmoil between the two religious factions still linger today. As recently as the 1990's, there were uprisings in Ulster, particularly Derry. The protest murals on Derry buildings near the dividing line with Londonderry serve as a silent reminder of the violent past. Northern Ireland remains governed by England, so their currency is Pound Sterling vs the Euros in southern Ireland. Many Irish would prefer to return to a unified Ireland. On my recent trip, we were reminded daily that there is only one Ireland, and that progress happens slowly.

The plantations and their related agricultural development radically altered Ireland's ecology and physical appearance. In 1600, most of Ireland was heavily wooded, apart from the bogs. Most of the population lived in small townlands, many migrating seasonally to fresh pastures for their cattle. By 1700, Ireland's native woodland had been decimated; it was intensively exploited by the new settlers for commercial ventures such as shipbuilding, as much of the English forests had been destroyed and the English navy was becoming a great power. Several native species, such as the wolf, were hunted to extinction during this period. The environmental adage that "whatever you do to the environment, you ultimately do to yourselves" came back to haunt the residents of Ireland, as the settler population became urbanized. Instead of many families growing and raising their own crops and livestock, they now relied on larger farms for the potatoes and grains for the people and livestock. The Irish Famine of 1740-41 was due to extremely cold and then rainy weather for successive years. Referred to as "The Great Frost", barely any snow fell, plus rivers, lakes, and waterfalls froze, causing fish to die. Frozen quays (pronounced "keys") temporarily kept ships from ferrying coal from south Wales, so there was no fuel for warming fires. People tried to avoid hypothermia without using up winter fuel reserves in a matter of days. Desperate people stripped bare hedges, ornamental trees, and nurseries around towns to obtain substitute fuel. The frozen rivers kept mill-wheels from operating, thus what stored grains that existed, could not be ground into wheat for baking. When the quays opened up at the end of January, coal prices soared, putting coal out of reach of most of the residents. By the summer of 1740, the Frost had decimated the potatoes, and the drought had destroyed the grain harvest. Herds of sheep and cattle died, causing a shortage of milk and meat. Starving rural dwellers started a "mass vagrancy" towards the better-supplied towns; by mid-June, beggars lined the streets. Arrest records from that era reflect the desperate measures these people resorted to, just to feed themselves and their families. An existing record from Londonderry, notes the arrest of one, James McGinnis on 30 March 1742, for the crime of "vagrancy", a term meaning a beggar or laborer seeking work. His punishment for this particular crime was deportation to America in 1745. Before you think too unhighly of James, remember the McGinnis clan lost their vast hereditary lands in 1690. This meant these McGinnis family members were left basically homeless... They survived by working on farms and other seasonal jobs. When the Famine hit, they became some of the aforementioned starving rural dwellers that became the street-lining beggars. Instead of the English Government aiding them by setting up shelters and food kitchens to house and feed these starving homeless...they arrested and gave them the choice of deportation or beheading. Horror stories about the ruthlessness of the Natives in America sadly caused many desperate early vagrants to choose death over deportation.

An estimated 400,000 persons died in Ireland during 1740-41. This prompted a mass migration to America, whereby Ulster lost close to a quarter of its population that had been engaged in manufacturing, to the new colony. Most of the earlier immigrants came through Philadelphia, which had a large population of English settlers. The English generally viewed these Ulster-Scot immigrants as their "dirty little cousins," due to their crudeness, and love of brawling. The Scots-Irish, realizing they could live a better life away from the British, followed a path westward, many to the rich Shenandoah Valley of Virginia. As word of the fertile lands spread back to Great Britain, many more Ulster-Scots departed Ireland and sailed to America. The first McGinnis in your line to leave the desperate times in Ireland, thankfully choosing deportation versus beheading, was the vagrant James McGinnis. Arriving in Virginia in 1750, he resided in Rockingham County until his death between 1760-65. Some of the Scots-Irish engaged in farming, but many more became tavern/hotel owners, mill operators, and general store operators. The battle-hardened Scots-Irish soon made an important contribution to the fledgling colony, as they were a valuable asset to the Continental Army in the Revolutionary War. Their wilderness experiences served them well in negotiating the wilds of America, including dealing with Native American attacks, and they needed little encouragement in attacking the much-hated elite British. Following your lineage, James McGinnis's son, James Baker McGinnis, born 1749 in Ireland, was a member of the Eleventh Regiment from 1775-1780. James B. eventually found his way to Richland Township in Venango County, where he passed away in 1836.

So – how did this Rev. War veteran find his way from Virginia to very rural Pennsylvania? Written records before 1880 are rare, so much of this may be rightfully viewed as speculation. The Donation Land program was used by the Commonwealth to induce men to stay in service during the Revolutionary War. Each Pennsylvania Line soldier and officer who served in the Continental forces until the end of the war was to receive a bounty, or donation, of a tract of land consisting of 200, 250, 350 or 500 acres, the size of the tract to be based upon his rank. The Donation Land area was located within the Purchase of 1784, immediately to the north of the Depreciation Lands and west of the Allegheny River, including parts of the counties of Butler, Clarion, Crawford, Erie, Lawrence, Mercer, Venango and Warren. I was able to find records that listed Robert McGinnis and Daniel McGinnis as recipients of 200 acres each of Venango County Donation Lands for their service. While there is no record for James, there is a record that states James B. filed a paper stating he should have been paid a stipend for his service and had never received the payment. He was awarded $.06 for each day that had passed to the date of filing. Is it possible the $33.30 in back payment was used to purchase property near his McGinnis relatives lands? Richland is a little further north than the actual Donation Lands, so it would not have been set aside for soldiers...and the name Robert is found in your lineage, and even James Baker's son was named Robert.

Marrying into Ulster-Scot lineage served to strengthen the Scots-Irish connections. While the Rugh line were of German heritage, the Jamisons, Sloans, Jolly's, and Wilson's were Ulster Scots. Famous relatives on the Voit lines include former Presidents Bill Clinton (8th cousin 3x removed) and George Washington (3rd cousin 7x removed), John Kerry (8th cousin 3x removed), Warren Buffett (11th cousin), Christina Aguilera (7th cousin 5x removed), Johnny Depp (6th cousin 5x removed), and Kurt Cobain (7th cousin 3x removed). Famous celebrities on the McGinnis line include Lady Gaga (8th cousin 4x removed), Evel Knieval (7th cousin 1x removed), and Benjamin Franklin (5th cousin 7x removed). Also on the McGinnis line, your 3 gr grandmother, Mary Ellen Jamison, is the link between your line and mine. We share a notable common ancestor in General Samuel Harvey Sloan.

Samuel Harvey Sloan, born in 1724 in Derry, Ireland, became one of the original western Pennsylvania pioneer settlers in what was to be Westmoreland County. The surname Sloan was derived from the Gaelic name Slaughan, which means "warrior". After immigrating from Ireland, our ancestor purchased land from the Penn family and settled in Hamilton Township, located in Cumberland County. He built and operated a grist mill, for which his name appears on the tax rolls as late as 1768. One of the founding fathers of Westmoreland County, Samuel arrived in the area that became Derry Township in 1769, and was one of the first to record property there. On April 3rd, 1769, he applied for a land patent of 320 acres called "Happy Discovery", which was located on the east side of the Loyalhanna Creek opposite the mouth of Fourteen Mile Run. This property later became part of the town of Latrobe.

The act, by which the County of Westmoreland was legislatively established, was passed on the 26th of February 1773. The next day the Governor sent to the Assembly a list of names that he had chosen, and whom he nominated as Justices of the County Courts. The Justices were commissioned under the broad seal of the Province of Pennsylvania, and of these twenty-six men, any three could hold court. Two of the twenty-six newly appointed Justices of the Courts of Westmoreland County were Samuel Sloan, Sr. and Robert Hanna.

Samuel Sloan, Sr. labored on such diverse tasks as dividing the county into townships and selecting Supervisors, laying out the new roads, selecting Constables, Sheriffs and Overseers of the Poor, naming members of a Grand Jury, recommending persons to sell "spirituous liquors" by small measure and setting the prices that the new tavern keepers could charge.

As soon as the place of justice had been fixed at Hanna's, a new one story, one room jail was built of rough hewn logs. Close by were erected a whipping post (where many a miscreant was whipped bloody and then salt was rubbed into their flesh) and a pillory, which was a framework raised from the ground and made with holes and folding doors through which the hands and head of the criminal were held in place. By common law, anybody passing a felon in the pillory could throw one stone at him.

Samuel Sloan, Sr. also helped to establish the Unity Presbyterian Church and Graveyard in 1774, received a land grant from the Penn Family for the same, and was one of the original Elders of the Church. He also contributed 10,000 Pounds Sterling to the Continental Army on June 2nd, 1780 and he also established Fort Sloan on his property for the protection of the settlers from the Indians. Samuel Sloan, Sr.'s monetary contribution to the Continental Army was never re-paid, and he was forced to sell some of his land in order to pay his taxes. He passed away on December 20, 1791.

Westmoreland County Colonial Flag

2013 marks the 240th Anniversary of the formation of Westmoreland County, PA. This Rattlesnake Flag, also known as the Proctor Flag, was designated the official flag of the County.
Tradition holds that the original rattlesnake flag was made in 1775 at Hanna's Town from a pre-existing British standard. The canton in the upper right hand corner consists of individual pieces of red, white, and blue silk, representing the English cross of St. George and the Scottish cross of St. Andrew. The retention of these British symbols on the flag indicates that the inhabitants of Westmoreland County, although ready to resist the tyrannical acts of the British Parliament, still considered themselves loyal subjects of King George III.
In the center of the field lies a rattlesnake coiled to strike. The snake's thirteen rattles signify the American colonies. The rattlesnake is painted directly on the silk, as is the lettering and decorative scroll work. Unlike on the earlier flags, the rattlesnake on the official flag is directly facing the symbol of the British Empire. Above the snake is the monogram of John Proctor and the letters I.B.W.C.P. This is believed to stand for Colonel John Proctor's 1st Battalion, Westmoreland County, Pennsylvania.

The terrains of both Scotland and, especially, Ireland are very suited to sheep farming. Thin, rocky soils on steep slopes with ample grasses, plus close proximity to climate modifying and moisture-producing oceans make for ideal stock raising conditions. For centuries, families relied on gardening near their homesteads for vegetables, and grazing sheep on the hillsides for meat and wool for clothing. Once World markets opened up, the Irish realized they could make a prosperous living by selling lamb and mutton to other countries, plus Irish wool became a desired product for weaving and clothing, and as such, commanded a hefty price on the World market. The Irish in Ulster became some of the wealthiest people in all of Great Britain, which was soon noticed by the English merchants. These merchants complained to the English government that they were unable to compete fairly with the wealthy Irish. True to past and future history, the Government of Great Britain took measures to control and dilute the wealth and power of the Irish merchants. Their solution was to pass legislation stating that the Irish merchants could no longer sell on the World market. Instead, the merchants could only sell their wool and meat to the English Government...and at a reduced price! Does this sound like the more familiar future Boston Tea Party? The regulations on meat and wool weren't about taxes, but about control. Is it any wonder the Scots and Irish hated the English?

The Stark Natural Beauty of Ulster...The Giant's Causeway

Formed around 50-60 million years ago when the area was subjected to intense volcanic activity. The molten basalt was forced through chalk beds to form a lava plateau. When it cooled, about 40,000 interlocking basalt columns were left. As the basalt weathered, the tops of the columns form stepping stones that lead from the cliff foot and disappear under the sea. In 2005, the site was named as the fourth greatest natural wonder in the United Kingdom

Located in County Antrim, on the northern coast of Ulster on the North Atlantic - the inlet that leads to Derry is located here. The distance between the northern coast of Antrim and the southern-most point in Scotland is only 12 miles. Our ancestors would have sailed past these basalt columns. Perhaps these columns would have been looked at as a symbol of pride - representing the strength and fortitude they would need to deal with unknown obstacles. One visit to an Irish pub, where musicians are playing folk music, will leave you with a deeper understanding of the pride the Irish have in their freedom, and the cost of that freedom.

Slieve League Sea Cliffs

The highest point of these cliffs reaches 1,972' – making them the highest in Europe. Our tour guide said the locals refer to these cliffs as being "twice the height" (as the Cliffs of Moher – their more famous cousin on the west coast of southern Ireland) – "and half the hype!"

If the cliffs along the island country of Ireland could talk, they would have a wealth of stories to relate. Shipwrecks from the Spanish Armada have been found off the northern coast, as well as Viking ships. Many people with Irish roots also have Scandinavian and Iberian Peninsula roots. Recent studies have shown that if a person has Irish or Scottish ancestry, and has red hair, they are likely of Viking descent. Because the gene for red hair is recessive, both parents would have to contribute that gene. These would be reflected in the DNA results. Other early invasions came from the Normans, located in present-day France and Belgium. So DNA results stating "Europe West" could be from this source.

Picturesque view of Irish terrain

Once wooded, this view gives you a better idea of the rough terrain, carved out by ancient glaciers, into which our ancestors laid out their plantations. The lighter green color in the bottom of the valley indicates a source of water for livestock, crops, and people alike. Remnants of the once-forested steep hillsides, are now plentiful lush grasslands, suitable for sure-footed ruminants. Who needs wooden fences when there is an abundance of stone? Similar rock walls are found in areas of America where the Irish settled, demonstrating one of many contributions our Irish ancestors made to America.

The Bridge of Tears

Approximately 6 miles from Dunfanaghy, there is an attractive little stone bridge, which most people pass over nowadays, without a second thought. But if you look more carefully, and pay attention to the nearby plaque, your curiosity may be raised somewhat. The plaque is written in Irish, and a rough translation into English would be, "Friends and relatives of the person emigrating would come this far. Here they parted. This is the Bridge of Tears".

Long before the building of the railway, or modern roads, this was the most common route leading from this area, to Derry, and hence to the ships which would take them to England, Scotland, Australia and America. The relatives of those emigrating would accompany them along the long walk up towards Muckish Gap, and here their Goodbyes would be said. There were no "See you soons" or "Catch you laters." The departure was treated like a death, for they would never be seen again. Crossing The Bridge had a finality for those who left, and for those who were left behind. And many tears were shed in this lonesome and beautiful place.

A simple plaque in stone beside the bridge reads:
"Fad leis seo a thagadh cairde agus lucht gaoil an té a bhí ag imeacht chun na coigrithe. B'anseo an scaradh. Seo Droichead na nDeor".
("Family and friends of the person leaving for foreign lands would come this far. Here was the separation. This is the Bridge of Tears".)

Present-day murals on the buildings depicting the turbulent history of Derry

Common Ancestors

Cousins	Common Ancestor	Possibilities
1	Grandparent	[illegible]
2	Great grandparent	[illegible]
3	2nd great grandparent	16
4	3rd great grandparent	[illegible]
5	4th great grandparent	[illegible]
6	5th great grandparent	[illegible]
7	6th great grandparent	256
8	7th great grandparent	512
9	8th great grandparent	1024
10	9th great grandparent	2048

Relationship Chart

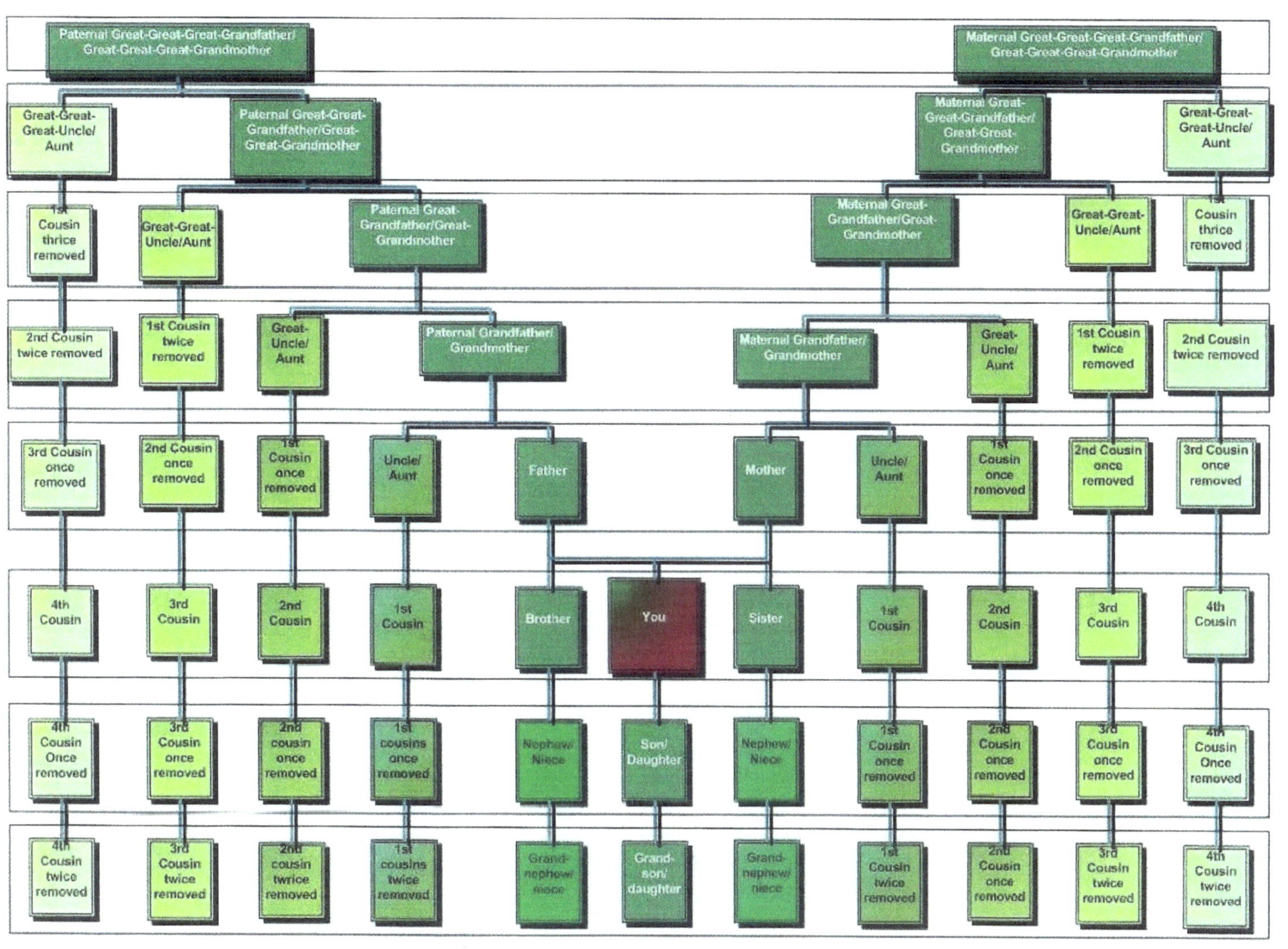

Scottish Naming Pattern

- First Born Son - named for the paternal grandfather
- Second Born Son - named for the maternal grandfather
- Third Son named for the father - unless he shares a name with one of the grandfathers
- Fourth and subsequent sons were often named after father or mother's brothers

- First Born Daughter - named for the maternal grandmother
- Second Born Daughter - named for the paternal grandmother
- Third Daughter - named for the mother - unless she shares a name with one of the grandmothers
- ·Subsequent daughters were generally named for mother or father's sisters

If one of the first three children died, often the next baby born of that same sex will be named after the baby that died.

Mary Ann McGinnis Pedigree Chart

How to read the following pages...The red arrows with a number at the right edge of the chart refer to the page where that family line is continued. The page numbers are in small print, found on the bottom center of each page.

Mr and Mrs Emery Voit 1968

(Mary Ann McGinnis)

Pedigree Chart for
Mary Ann McGinnis

| Parents | Grandparents | Great-Grandparents |

Charles Richard McGinnis
- b: 29 Aug 1852 in Salem Twp Clarion County, Pennsylvania
- m: 21 Feb 1878 in Scrubgrass Church Venago Co. Pa.
- d: 12 Dec 1939 in Salem, Clarion, Pennsylvania, USA
- Cause Of Death: ; Chronic Nephritis

Robert W McGinnis → 2
- b: 10 Aug 1800 in Northumberl...
- m: of PA
- d: 24 Aug 1881 in Salem, Clari...
- Cause Of Death:

Elizabeth Jane Layton → 3
- b: 02 Sep 1815 in Scrubgrass, Venango, Pennsylvania, USA
- d: 09 Mar 1896 in Salem, Clarion, Pennsylvania, USA
- Cause Of Death:

Roland B. McGinnis
- b: 12 Feb 1879 in Allegheny Township Butler County, Pennsylvania
- m: 26 Jan 1907 in Clarion, Pennsylvania, USA
- d: 11 Feb 1946 in Oil City, Venango, PA
- Cause Of Death: ; Heart Attack - Blood clot

Mary Ellen Jamison
- b: 30 Nov 1859 in Scrubgrass Twp.Venango Co Pa
- d: 23 Apr 1932 in Lamartine, Clarion, Pennsylvania, United States
- Cause Of Death: ; Chronic Nephritis

George S Jamison → 4
- b: 02 Dec 1816 in Huntingdon...
- m: 1849 in Butler, Butler, Penns...
- d: 22 May 1883 in Scrubgrass T...
- Cause Of Death:

Elizabeth Betsy Jolly → 5
- b: 06 Oct 1824 in Butler County,Pa
- d: 24 Jan 1910 in Eau Claire,Butler Co.,Pa
- Cause Of Death: ; Senility

Mary Ann McGinnis
- b: 08 Jun 1915 in Lamberton, PA
- m:
- d: 18 Jul 1974 in Oil City, Venango, PA
- Cause Of Death: ; Heart Attack

Emanuel Jonas Rugh
- b: 15 Feb 1845 in Salem, Clarion, Pennsylvania, USA
- m: 10 Jan 1867 in Clarion,Clarion,Pennsylvania,USA
- d: 24 Aug 1939 in Salem Township,Clarion,Pennsylvania,USA
- Cause Of Death: ; Chronic Nephritis ...Enlarged prostate

William Rugh → 6
- b: 19 Oct 1801 in Rugh`s Stati...
- m: Mar 1829 in Blairsville, India...
- d: 10 Apr 1886 in Salem, Clario...
- Cause Of Death:

Charlotte Susan Mikesell → 7
- b: 10 Jan 1806 in Armstrong,Ind...
- d: 12 Aug 1883 in Salem, Clari...
- Cause Of Death:

Effie Erletta Rugh
- b: 14 May 1878 in Lamartine, Clarion County, Pennsylvania, USA
- d: 23 Mar 1963 in Lamartine, Clarion, Pennsylvania, United States
- Cause Of Death: ; Car accident

Clara Ann Kuhns
- b: 28 Mar 1845 in Clarion County, Pennsylvania, United States of America
- d: 17 Feb 1913 in Clarion County, Pennsylvania, United States of America
- Cause Of Death: ; Apoplexy (stroke)

John Kiser Kuhns → 8
- b: 19 Feb 1824 in Lampeter Township
- m:
- d: 1904
- Cause Of Death:

Maria McGinnis
- b: Jan 1826 in PA
- d: 1846 in PA
- Cause Of Death:

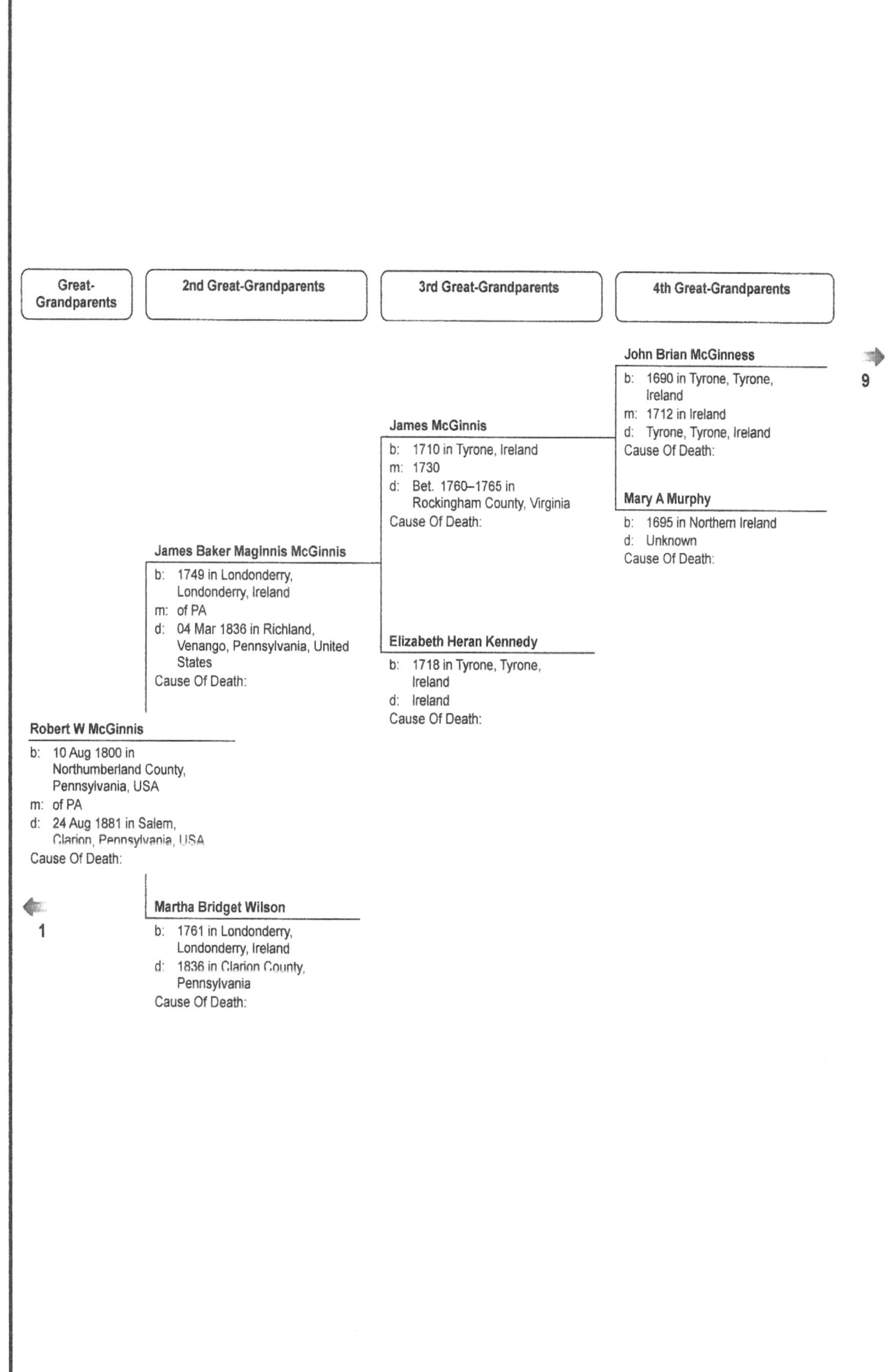

Great-Grandparents	2nd Great-Grandparents	3rd Great-Grandparents	4th Great-Grandparents

John Brian McGinness

b: 1690 in Tyrone, Tyrone, Ireland
m: 1712 in Ireland
d: Tyrone, Tyrone, Ireland
Cause Of Death:

9

James McGinnis

b: 1710 in Tyrone, Ireland
m: 1730
d: Bet. 1760–1765 in Rockingham County, Virginia
Cause Of Death:

Mary A Murphy

b: 1695 in Northern Ireland
d: Unknown
Cause Of Death:

James Baker Maginnis McGinnis

b: 1749 in Londonderry, Londonderry, Ireland
m: of PA
d: 04 Mar 1836 in Richland, Venango, Pennsylvania, United States
Cause Of Death:

Elizabeth Heran Kennedy

b: 1718 in Tyrone, Tyrone, Ireland
d: Ireland
Cause Of Death:

Robert W McGinnis

b: 10 Aug 1800 in Northumberland County, Pennsylvania, USA
m: of PA
d: 24 Aug 1881 in Salem, Clarion, Pennsylvania, USA
Cause Of Death:

1

Martha Bridget Wilson

b: 1761 in Londonderry, Londonderry, Ireland
d: 1836 in Clarion County, Pennsylvania
Cause Of Death:

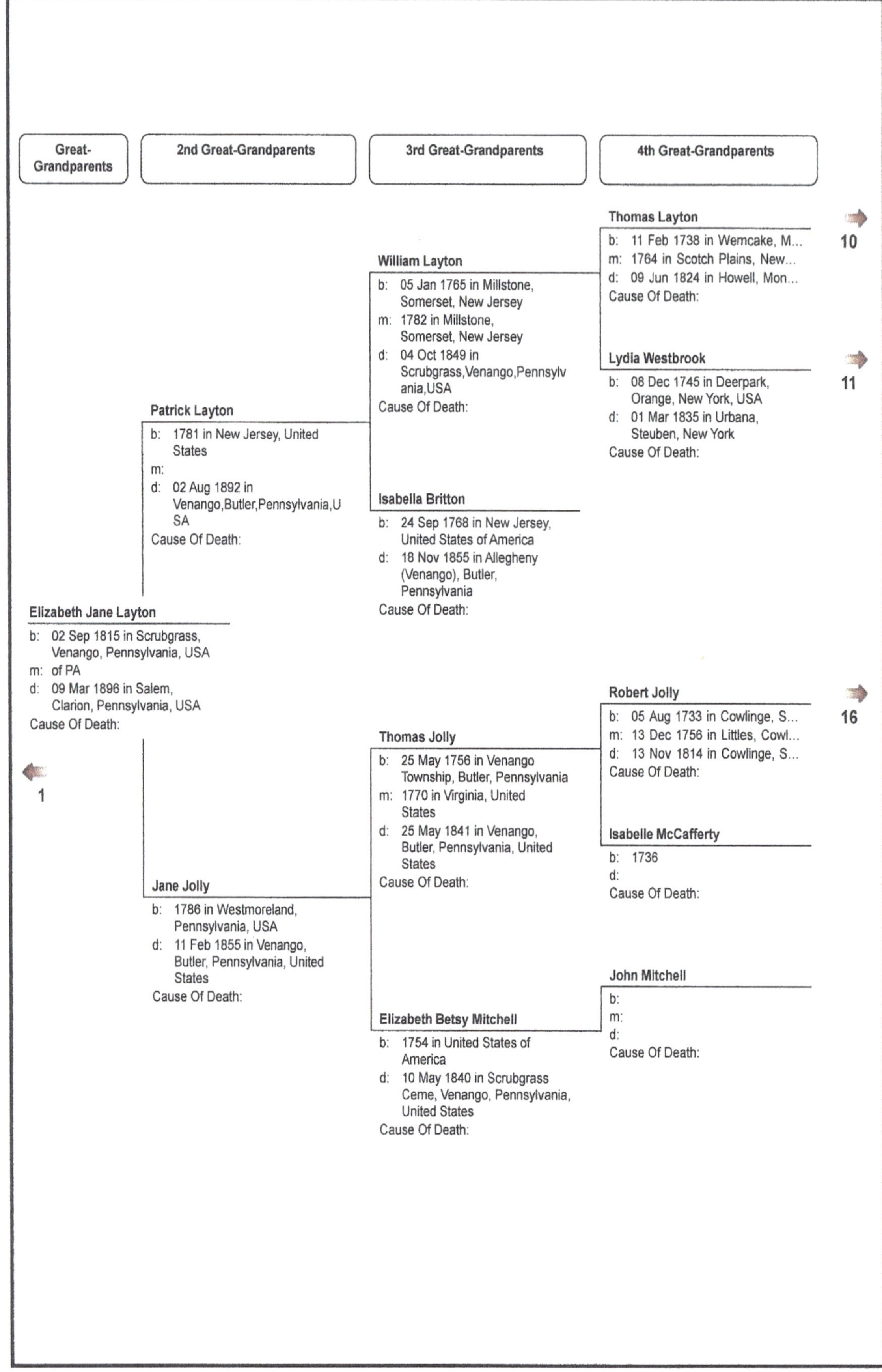

Great-Grandparents

2nd Great-Grandparents

3rd Great-Grandparents

4th Great-Grandparents

Thomas Layton
b: 11 Feb 1738 in Wemcake, M...
m: 1764 in Scotch Plains, New...
d: 09 Jun 1824 in Howell, Mon...
Cause Of Death:
10

William Layton
b: 05 Jan 1765 in Millstone,
Somerset, New Jersey
m: 1782 in Millstone,
Somerset, New Jersey
d: 04 Oct 1849 in
Scrubgrass,Venango,Pennsylv
ania,USA
Cause Of Death:

Lydia Westbrook
b: 08 Dec 1745 in Deerpark,
Orange, New York, USA
d: 01 Mar 1835 in Urbana,
Steuben, New York
Cause Of Death:
11

Patrick Layton
b: 1781 in New Jersey, United
States
m:
d: 02 Aug 1892 in
Venango,Butler,Pennsylvania,U
SA
Cause Of Death:

Isabella Britton
b: 24 Sep 1768 in New Jersey,
United States of America
d: 18 Nov 1855 in Allegheny
(Venango), Butler,
Pennsylvania
Cause Of Death:

Elizabeth Jane Layton
b: 02 Sep 1815 in Scrubgrass,
Venango, Pennsylvania, USA
m: of PA
d: 09 Mar 1896 in Salem,
Clarion, Pennsylvania, USA
Cause Of Death:
1

Robert Jolly
b: 05 Aug 1733 in Cowlinge, S...
m: 13 Dec 1756 in Littles, Cowl...
d: 13 Nov 1814 in Cowlinge, S...
Cause Of Death:
16

Thomas Jolly
b: 25 May 1756 in Venango
Township, Butler, Pennsylvania
m: 1770 in Virginia, United
States
d: 25 May 1841 in Venango,
Butler, Pennsylvania, United
States
Cause Of Death:

Isabelle McCafferty
b: 1736
d:
Cause Of Death:

Jane Jolly
b: 1786 in Westmoreland,
Pennsylvania, USA
d: 11 Feb 1855 in Venango,
Butler, Pennsylvania, United
States
Cause Of Death:

John Mitchell
b:
m:
d:
Cause Of Death:

Elizabeth Betsy Mitchell
b: 1754 in United States of
America
d: 10 May 1840 in Scrubgrass
Ceme, Venango, Pennsylvania,
United States
Cause Of Death:

Great-Grandparents	2nd Great-Grandparents	3rd Great-Grandparents	4th Great-Grandparents

Alexander Jamison

b: 1700 in Ulster, Ireland
m: 30 Sep 1727 in Philadelphia,...
d: Mar 1749 in Warwick, Bucks,...
Cause Of Death:

13

John Jamison

b: 1748 in Aberdenshire, Scotland
m: Abt. 1788 in Westmoreland, Pennsylvania, United States
d: 25 Jun 1839 in Marion, Butler, Pennsylvania, United States
Cause Of Death:

Martha G. Richey

b: 1705 in Ireland
d: 1760 in Warwick, Bucks, Pennsylvania, United States
Cause Of Death:

14

John S. Jamison

b: 22 Mar 1785 in Somerset County, Pennsylvania, USA
m: 11 Jun 1811 in Sinking Creek Church, Centre, Pennsylvania, United States
d: 25 Mar 1869 in Venango Township; Venango County, Pennsylvania
Cause Of Death:

Janette Garth

b: 1750 in Ireland
d: 17 Apr 1822 in Butler, Pennsylvania, United States
Cause Of Death:

George S Jamison

b: 02 Dec 1816 in Huntingdon Co. Pa
m: 1849 in Butler, Butler, Pennsylvania, United States
d: 22 May 1883 in Scrubgrass Twp. Venango Co Pa
Cause Of Death:

1

Hooker Kuhns

b: 1725 in Hanau, Main-Kinzig-...
m:
d: Abt. 1800 in Youngstown, U...
Cause Of Death:

Henry (Heinrich) Nicholas Kuhn (Koone)

b: 1749 in Kilianstaedten, , Germany
m: 1777 in Berks County, Pennsylvania, USA
d: 04 Apr 1838 in Youngstown, Westmoreland County, Pennsylvania, USA
Cause Of Death:

M M Miller

b: Abt. 1730
d: Abt. 1800 in St James Cemetery, Youngstown, Unity Twnship, Westmoreland Co, PA
Cause Of Death:

Mary Kuhn

b: 20 Apr 1788 in Pennsylvania, United States
d: 13 Dec 1869 in Cherry Valley (Butler County), Butler County, Pennsylvania, USA
Cause Of Death:

George Adam Leibensperger

b: 29 Sep 1726 in Niederbronn...
m: 26 Sep 1749 in New Hanove...
d: 26 Sep 1799 in Maxatawny,...
Cause Of Death:

15

Ana Catharina Leibensperger

b: 01 Sep 1751 in Weisenburg, Bucks, Pennsylvania, United States
d: 06 May 1841 in Youngstown, Westmoreland, Pennsylvania, United States
Cause Of Death:

Catharina Barbara Kuhntz

b: 13 Jan 1727 in Niederbronn,...
d: 25 Sep 1809 in Maxatawny,...
Cause Of Death:

Robert Jolly → 12
b: 05 Aug 1733 in Cowlinge, S...
m: 13 Dec 1756 in Littles, Cowl...
d: 13 Nov 1814 in Cowlinge, S...
Cause Of Death:

Thomas Jolly
b: 25 May 1756 in Venango Township, Butler, Pennsylvania
m: 1770 in Virginia, United States
d: 25 May 1841 in Venango, Butler, Pennsylvania, United States
Cause Of Death:

Isabelle McCafferty
b: 1736
d:
Cause Of Death:

James Jolly
b: 1798 in Venango, Butler, Pennsylvania, United States
m:
d: Aug 1829
Cause Of Death:

John Mitchell
b:
m:
d:
Cause Of Death:

Elizabeth Betsy Mitchell
b: 1754 in United States of America
d: 10 May 1840 in Scrubgrass Ceme, Venango, Pennsylvania, United States
Cause Of Death:

Elizabeth Betsy Jolly
b: 06 Oct 1824 in Butler County,Pa
m: 1849 in Butler, Butler, Pennsylvania, United States
d: 24 Jan 1910 in Eau Claire,Butler Co.,Pa
Cause Of Death: ; Senility

← 1

Gen. Samuel Harvy Sloan Sr. → 17
b: 1724 in Derry, Ireland
m: 1747 in Saitfield,Co.Down,...
d: 20 Dec 1791 in Latrobe, W...
Cause Of Death:

Samuel Sloan
b: 1763 in Green, Cumberland, Pennsylvania, United States
m: 1789 in Westmoreland, Jamaica
d: 13 Apr 1837 in Venango, Butler, Pennsylvania
Cause Of Death:

Agnes Ann Clarke Carnahan
b: 1724 in Belfast, Ireland
d: 1790 in Unity, Westmoreland, Pennsylvania, United States
Cause Of Death:

Jane Sloan
b: 06 Oct 1800 in Venango, Butler, Pennsylvania, United States
d: 18 Jun 1879 in Venango, Butler, Pennsylvania, United States
Cause Of Death:

John Bran → 18
b: 1740 in Virginia, United States
m: 1765
d: 1782 in Derry, Westmorelan...
Cause Of Death:

Rebecca Elizabeth Bran
b: 1765 in Pennsylvania, United States
d: 02 Jun 1837 in Venango, Butler, Pennsylvania, United States
Cause Of Death:

Elizabeth Oliver
b: 1744
d: Pennsylvania
Cause Of Death:

John Michael Rugh → **19**
b: 05 Jan 1723 in Gumbrechtsh...
m: 16 Apr 1745 in Moselem, Pe...
d: 28 Mar 1820 in Franklin, W...
Cause Of Death:

Johann Peter (John Peter) Rugh Sr.
b: 17 Aug 1747 in Northampton County, Pennsylvania, USA
m: 1770 in Westmoreland, Pennsylvania, United States
d: 22 Dec 1828 in Greensburg, Westmoreland, Pennsylvania, USA
Cause Of Death:

Anna Frantzina Merckling → **20**
b: 11 Feb 1717 in Ludwigshafen...
d: 13 Jul 1782 in Hannastown,...
Cause Of Death:

Christopher Christian R Rugh
b: 20 Jun 1773 in Hempfield, Westmoreland, Pennsylvania, United States
m: Abt. 1796 in Westmoreland, Pennsylvania, United States
d: 20 Mar 1835 in Burrell, Indiana, Pennsylvania, United States
Cause Of Death:

Johan Ludwig Keister
b: 18 Sep 1723 in Durstel, Bas-...
m: 04 Nov 1748 in Bettwiler, Als...
d: 11 Dec 1786 in Leigh, Northa...
Cause Of Death:

Anna Maria Margaretha Keister
b: 11 Dec 1753 in Durstel, Bas-Rhin, Alsace, France
d: 12 Apr 1831 in Greensburg, Westmoreland, Pennsylvania, USA
Cause Of Death:

Eva Christina Antoni
b: 12 May 1723 in Bettwiller, Bas-Rhin, Alsace, France
d: 1786 in Lehigh, Northampton Co, Pennsylvania
Cause Of Death:

William Rugh
b: 19 Oct 1801 in Rugh`s Station, Burrell Township, Indiana County, Pennsylvania, USA
m: Mar 1829 in Blairsville, Indiana, Pennsylvania, United States
d: 10 Apr 1886 in Salem, Clarion County, Pennsylvania, USA

Cause Of Death:

← **1**

Johan Wilhelm Best Jr
b: 30 Nov 1713 in Switzerland,...
m: 1732 in Palatinate, Rhine, G...
d: 24 Nov 1762 in Lehigh, Nort...
Cause Of Death:

Cap. Johan Wilhelm Best
b: 1733 in Palatinate, Rheinland-Pfalz, Germany
m: 1762 in Westmoreland, Pennsylvania, United States
d: 1823 in Beaver City, Clarion, Pennsylvania, United States
Cause Of Death:

Anna Susanna Schaeffer
b: 1717 in Pfungstadt, Darmsta...
d: 1769 in Lehigh, Northampton...
Cause Of Death:

Anna Elizabeth Best
b: 13 Feb 1776 in Harrolds Church, Westmoreland, Pennsylvania, United States
d: 08 May 1841 in Center Township, Indiana County, Pennsylvaniaj
Cause Of Death:

Johann George Hawk or Hauck or Haag
b: 1710 in Westmoreland,,Pen...
m: 1741 in Germany
d: 1798 in Lehigh, Northampton...
Cause Of Death:

Anna Catherine Hawk
b: 1735 in Reutlingen, Reutlingen, Baden-Wuerttemberg, Germany
d: 1786 in Hempfield, Westmoreland, Pennsylvania, United States
Cause Of Death:

Catharina Hanselmann
b: 1712 in , , , Germany
d: 1809 in Pennsylvania, Somerset, Pennsylvania, USA
Cause Of Death:

<table>
<tr><td>Great-
Grandparents</td><td>2nd Great-Grandparents</td><td>3rd Great-Grandparents</td><td>4th Great-Grandparents</td></tr>
</table>

Johann Jacob Meixell   21
b: 14 Jun 1705 in Heidelberg, L…
m: 1730 in Conestoga, Lancast…
d: 18 Jan 1759 in Williams, N…
Cause Of Death:

Johannes John Meixell
b: 04 Oct 1733 in Muddy
   Creek, Lancaster Co., PA
m:
d: 29 Oct 1808 in Frantz
   School Cemetery Ross Twp.
   Monroe Co. PA
Cause Of Death:

Anna Margaret Maria Kitzmiller   22
b: 1709 in Leimen, Rhein-Neck…
d: 1805 in Leiman, , Baden-W…
Cause Of Death:

John Mikesell
b: 1769 in Chestnut Hill,
   Northampton Co,
   Pennsylvania, USA
m: 1793 in
   Hamilton,Northampton,Pennsyl
   vania,USA
d: 22 Aug 1826 in Center,
   Indiana, Pennsylvania, United
   States
Cause Of Death:

Anna Margaretha Illig
b: 14 Oct 1738 in Lower
   Saucon, Northampton,
   Pennsylvania, United States
d: 30 May 1797 in Chestnut
   Hill, Monroe, Pennsylvania,
   United States
Cause Of Death:

Charlotte Susan Mikesell
b: 10 Jan 1806 in
   Armstrong,Indiana,Pennsylvani
   a,USA
m: Mar 1829 in Blairsville,
   Indiana, Pennsylvania, United
   States
d: 12 Aug 1883 in Salem,
   Clarion, Pennsylvania, United
   States
Cause Of Death:

1

Hans Peter Altomus
b: 24 Oct 1700 in Hundheim, A…
m:
d: 1748 in Philadelphia, Delawa…
Cause Of Death:

Nicholas A. Altimus
b: 30 Apr 1745 in Philadelphia,
   Philadelphia, Pennsylvania,
   USA
m: 1770
d: 02 Jul 1836 in Chestnuthill,
   Northampton, Pennsylvania,
   USA
Cause Of Death:

Elisabetha Catharina Wildtberger
b: 1700 in Oppelsbohm, Germa…
d: 1748 in Philadelphia, Philad…
Cause Of Death:

Margaretha Elisabeth Altemus
b: 15 Apr 1771 in Hamilton
   Twp, Northampton,
   Pennsylvania, United States
d: 30 Jan 1854 in Center
   Township,Indiana,Pennsylvania
   ,USA
Cause Of Death:

Henry Frantz
b: 15 Nov 1716 in Diedendorf,…
m: 23 Jun 1744 in Rauwiller,,,G…
d: Mar 1777 in , Northampton,…
Cause Of Death:

Schalotta Juliana Frantz Altemus
b: Jan 1747 in Chestnuthill,
   Northampton, Pennsylvania,
   USA
d: 15 Sep 1806 in Saylorsburg,
   Northampton, Pennsylvania,
   USA
Cause Of Death:

Susanna Girardin
b: 19 Mar 1727 in Diedendorf,
   Bas-Rhin, Alsace, France
d: Jan 1782 in , Northampton,
   Pennsylvania, USA
Cause Of Death:

Great-Grandparents	2nd Great-Grandparents	3rd Great-Grandparents	4th Great-Grandparents

Johann Jacob Kuhn
b: Sep 1710 in Haardt, Rheinla…
m: 31 Aug 1739 in Haardt, Rhei…
d: 13 Apr 1781 in Haardt, Rhein…
Cause Of Death:

Bartholomew Kuhns
b: 1741 in Rheinland-Pfalz, Germany
m:
d: 1774 in Pennsylvania, United States
Cause Of Death:

Anna Margaretha Köhler
b: 11 Jul 1700 in Haardt, Rheinland-Pfalz, Germany
d: 22 Feb 1758 in Haardt, Rheinland-Pfalz, Germany
Cause Of Death:

John Christian Kuhns
b: 02 Feb 1787 in Westmoreland, Pennsylvania, United States
m: 1808
d: 03 Mar 1862 in Shippenville, Clarion, Pennsylvania, USA
Cause Of Death:

George Christian Heisler
b: 1702 in Niederhofen, Alb-Do…
m: 03 Feb 1728 in Neckarwesth…
d: 21 Jun 1799 in Ralpho, Lanc…
Cause Of Death:

Anna Christina Heisler
b: 1746 in Niederhofen, Alb-Donau-Kreis, Baden-Wuerttemberg, Germany
d: 1796 in Pennsylvania, United States
Cause Of Death:

Eva Elizabeth Menius
b: 1710 in Baden-Württemberg, Germany
d: 1749 in Ralpho, Lancaster, Pennsylvania, United States
Cause Of Death:

John Kiser Kuhns
b: 19 Feb 1824 in Lampeter Township
m:
d: 1904
Cause Of Death:

1

Johann Peter Keiser
b: 28 Oct 1726 in Palitine, West…
m: 1751 in Longswamp, Berks,…
d: 16 Apr 1804 in Macungie, N…
Cause Of Death:

Johann Peter (known as Peter) Kiser Sr.
b: 15 Jan 1759 in Macungie, Northampton, Pennsylvania, USA
m: 1785 in Northampton. Pennsylvania, USA
d: 11 Nov 1829 in Shippenville, Clarion, Pennsylvania, United States
Cause Of Death:

Anna Margaretha
b: 1740 in Longswamp, Berks, Pennsylvania, United States
d: 1793 in Northhampton, Pennsylvania, United States
Cause Of Death:

Sarah Elizabeth Kiser
b: 04 Jun 1787 in Upper Milford, Northampton, Pennsylvania, United States
d: 06 Feb 1867 in Shippenville, Clarion, Pennsylvania, United States
Cause Of Death:

Captain David Strauss
b: 27 Dec 1734 in Diez, Rhein-…
m: 21 Aug 1761 in Pastor, Santi…
d: 04 Mar 1826 in Hamilton, M…
Cause Of Death:

Anna Margaretha (Mary) Strauss
b: 22 May 1764 in Diez, Rhein-Lahn-Kreis, Rheinland-Pfalz, Germany
d: 16 Oct 1850 in Shippenville, Clarion, Pennsylvania, United States,
Cause Of Death:

Anna Maria Philippina Roscher
b: 23 Aug 1739 in Diez, Rhein-…
d: 24 Sep 1825 in Hamilton, M…
Cause Of Death:

<table>
<tr><td>4th Great-
Grandparents</td><td>5th Great-Grandparents</td></tr>
</table>

Hugh McGennis

b: 1645 in Ireland
m:
d: Ireland
Cause Of Death:

John Brian McGinness

b: 1690 in Tyrone, Tyrone,
   Ireland
m: 1712 in Ireland
d: Tyrone, Tyrone, Ireland
Cause Of Death:

2

Andrew Layton

b: 1698 in Wemcake,
Monmouth, New Jersey
m: 1713 in Piscataway,
Middlesex, New Jersey, United
States
d: 1765 in Wemcake,
Monmouth, New Jersey
Cause Of Death:

Thomas Layton

b: 11 Feb 1738 in Wemcake,
Monmouth, New Jersey, USA
m: 1764 in Scotch Plains, New
Jersey
d: 09 Jun 1824 in Howell,
Monmouth County, New Jersey,
United States of America
Cause Of Death:

3

Margaret Dunn

b: 10 Apr 1700 in Monmouth,
New Jersey, United States
d: 1781 in Wemcake,
Monmonth County, NJ
Cause Of Death:

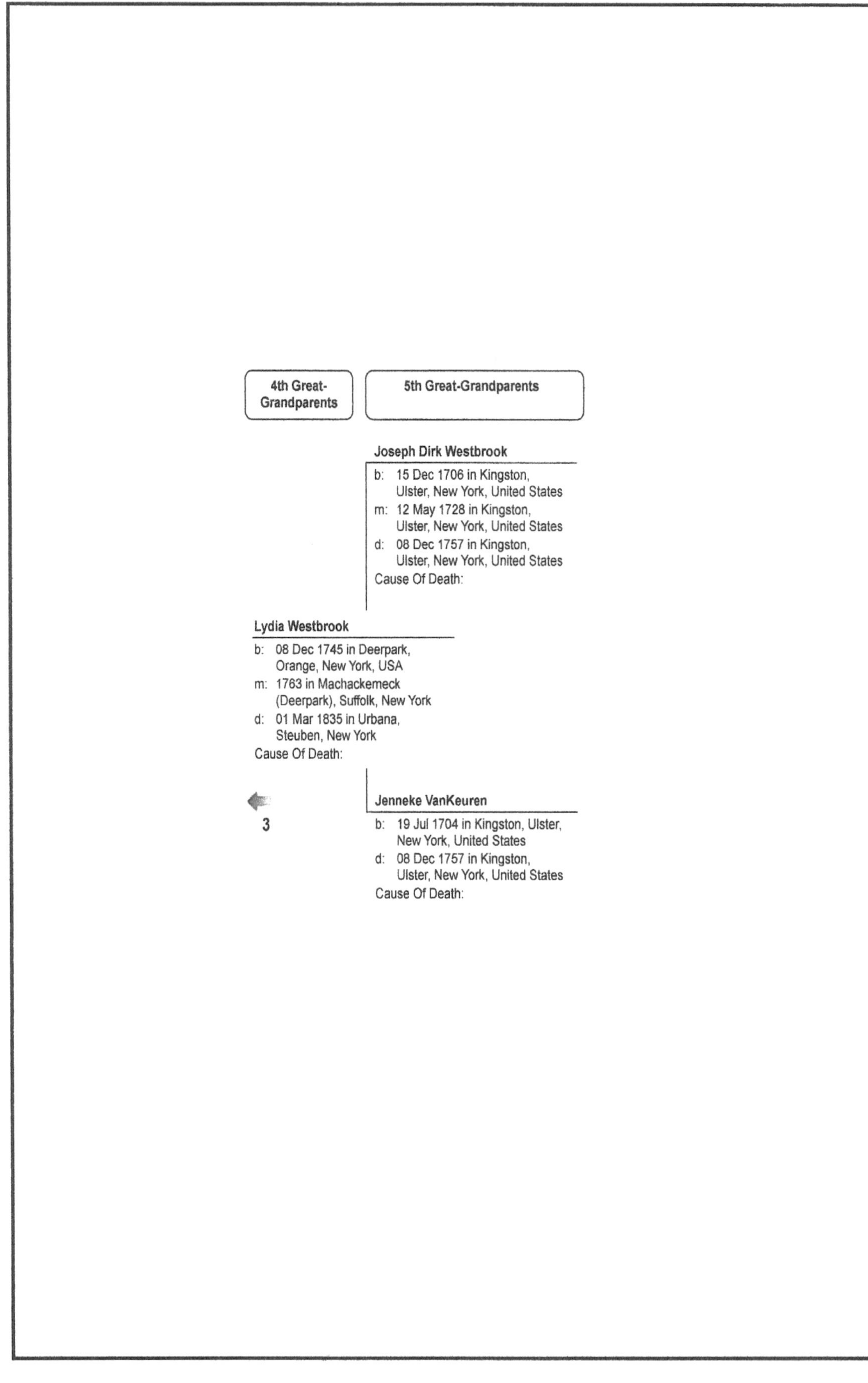

4th Great-Grandparents

5th Great-Grandparents

Joseph Dirk Westbrook
b: 15 Dec 1706 in Kingston,
    Ulster, New York, United States
m: 12 May 1728 in Kingston,
    Ulster, New York, United States
d: 08 Dec 1757 in Kingston,
    Ulster, New York, United States
Cause Of Death:

Lydia Westbrook
b: 08 Dec 1745 in Deerpark,
    Orange, New York, USA
m: 1763 in Machackemeck
    (Deerpark), Suffolk, New York
d: 01 Mar 1835 in Urbana,
    Steuben, New York
Cause Of Death:

3

Jenneke VanKeuren
b: 19 Jul 1704 in Kingston, Ulster,
    New York, United States
d: 08 Dec 1757 in Kingston,
    Ulster, New York, United States
Cause Of Death:

Henry Jolly

b: 19 Jul 1692 in Lidgate,
Suffolk, England
m: 17 Nov 1715 in Lidgate,
Suffolk, England
d: 13 Feb 1770 in Cowlinge,
Suffolk, England
Cause Of Death:

Robert Jolly

b: 05 Aug 1733 in Cowlinge,
Suffolk, England
m: 13 Dec 1756 in Littles,
Cowlinge, Suffolk, England
d: 13 Nov 1814 in Cowlinge,
Suffolk, England
Cause Of Death:

5

Rebecca Anthony

b: Abt. 1694 in Cowlinge,
Suffolk, England
d: 30 May 1749 in Cowlinge,
Suffolk, England
Cause Of Death:

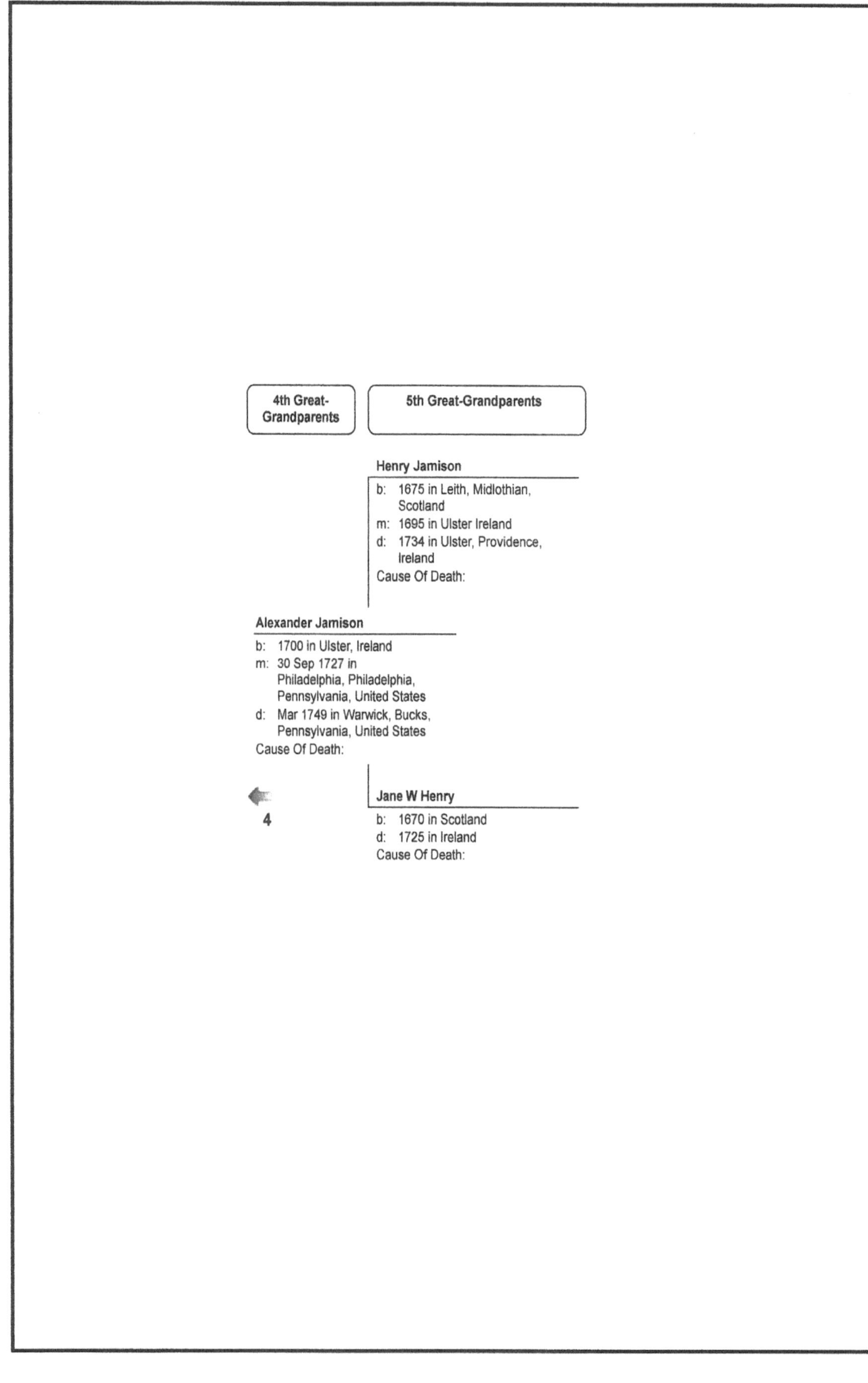

4th Great-Grandparents

5th Great-Grandparents

Henry Jamison
b: 1675 in Leith, Midlothian, Scotland
m: 1695 in Ulster Ireland
d: 1734 in Ulster, Providence, Ireland
Cause Of Death:

Alexander Jamison
b: 1700 in Ulster, Ireland
m: 30 Sep 1727 in Philadelphia, Philadelphia, Pennsylvania, United States
d: Mar 1749 in Warwick, Bucks, Pennsylvania, United States
Cause Of Death:

4

Jane W Henry
b: 1670 in Scotland
d: 1725 in Ireland
Cause Of Death:

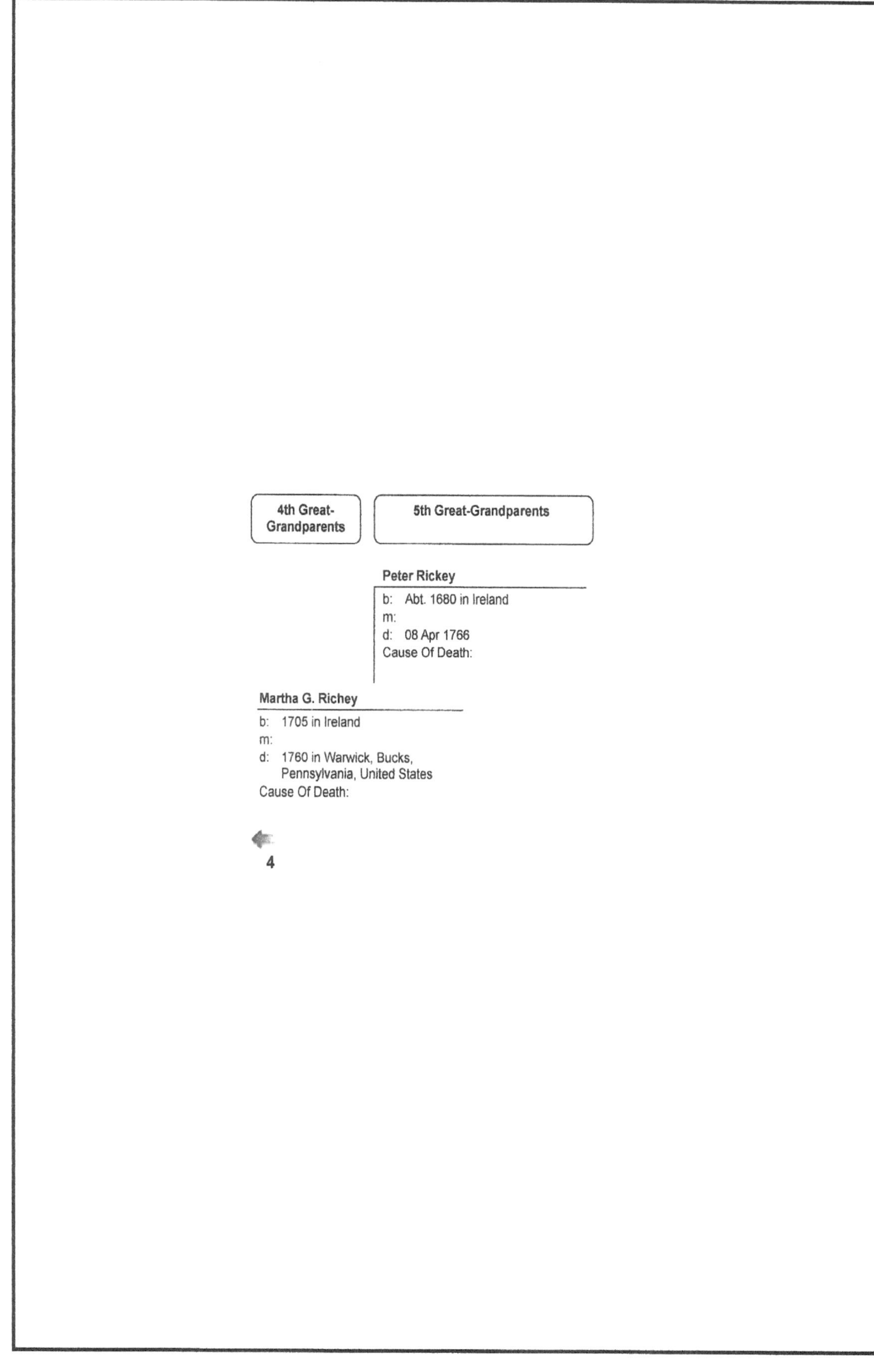
4th Great-
Grandparents

5th Great-Grandparents

Peter Rickey
b: Abt. 1680 in Ireland
m:
d: 08 Apr 1766
Cause Of Death:

Martha G. Richey
b: 1705 in Ireland
m:
d: 1760 in Warwick, Bucks,
      Pennsylvania, United States
Cause Of Death:

4

Johann John "Hans" George Leibensperger

b: 05 Aug 1693 in Ilshofen, Schwäbisch Hall, Baden-Württemberg, Germany
m:
d: 1767 in Weisenberg Township, Lehigh County, Pennsylvania, USA
Cause Of Death:

George Adam Leibensperger

b: 29 Sep 1726 in Niederbronn-les-Bains, France
m: 26 Sep 1749 in New Hanover, Montgomery, Pennsylvania, United States
d: 26 Sep 1799 in Maxatawny, Berks, Pennsylvania, United States
Cause Of Death:

4

Mary

b: Ilshofen, Schwäbisch Hall, Baden-Württemberg, Germany
d: 1767 in Weisenberg Township, Lehigh County, Pennsylvania, USA
Cause Of Death:

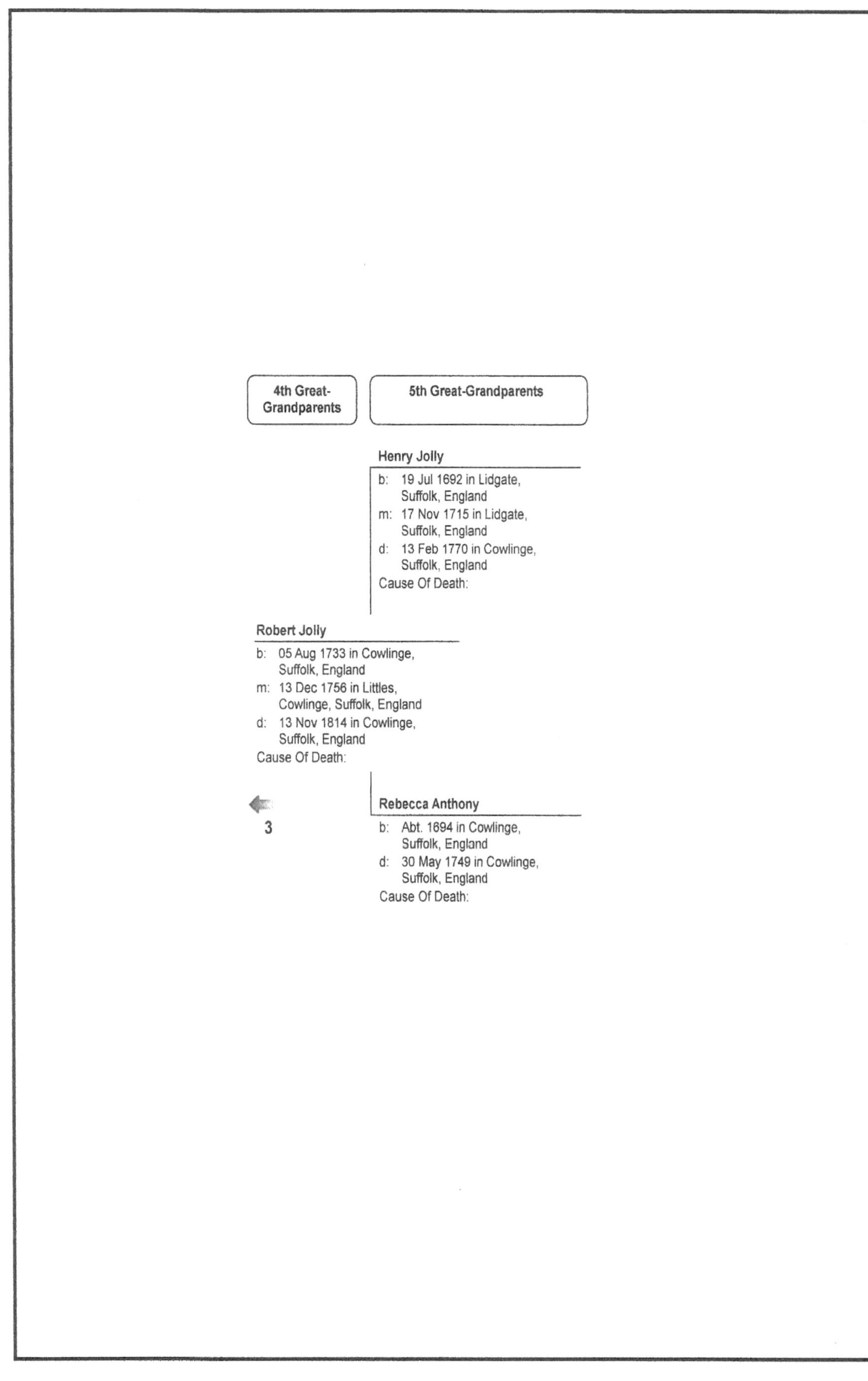

4th Great-Grandparents

5th Great-Grandparents

Henry Jolly
b: 19 Jul 1692 in Lidgate,
     Suffolk, England
m: 17 Nov 1715 in Lidgate,
     Suffolk, England
d: 13 Feb 1770 in Cowlinge,
     Suffolk, England
Cause Of Death:

Robert Jolly
b: 05 Aug 1733 in Cowlinge,
     Suffolk, England
m: 13 Dec 1756 in Littles,
     Cowlinge, Suffolk, England
d: 13 Nov 1814 in Cowlinge,
     Suffolk, England
Cause Of Death:

3

Rebecca Anthony
b: Abt. 1694 in Cowlinge,
     Suffolk, England
d: 30 May 1749 in Cowlinge,
     Suffolk, England
Cause Of Death:

<table>
<tr><td>4th Great-
Grandparents</td><td>5th Great-Grandparents</td></tr>
</table>

Gen. Samuel Harvy Sloan Sr.

b: 1724 in Derry, Ireland
m: 1747 in Saitfield,Co.Down,
   No. Ireland
d: 20 Dec 1791 in Latrobe,
   Westmoreland County,
   Pennsylvania, USA
Cause Of Death:

5

Nancy Tate

b:
m:
d:
Cause Of Death:

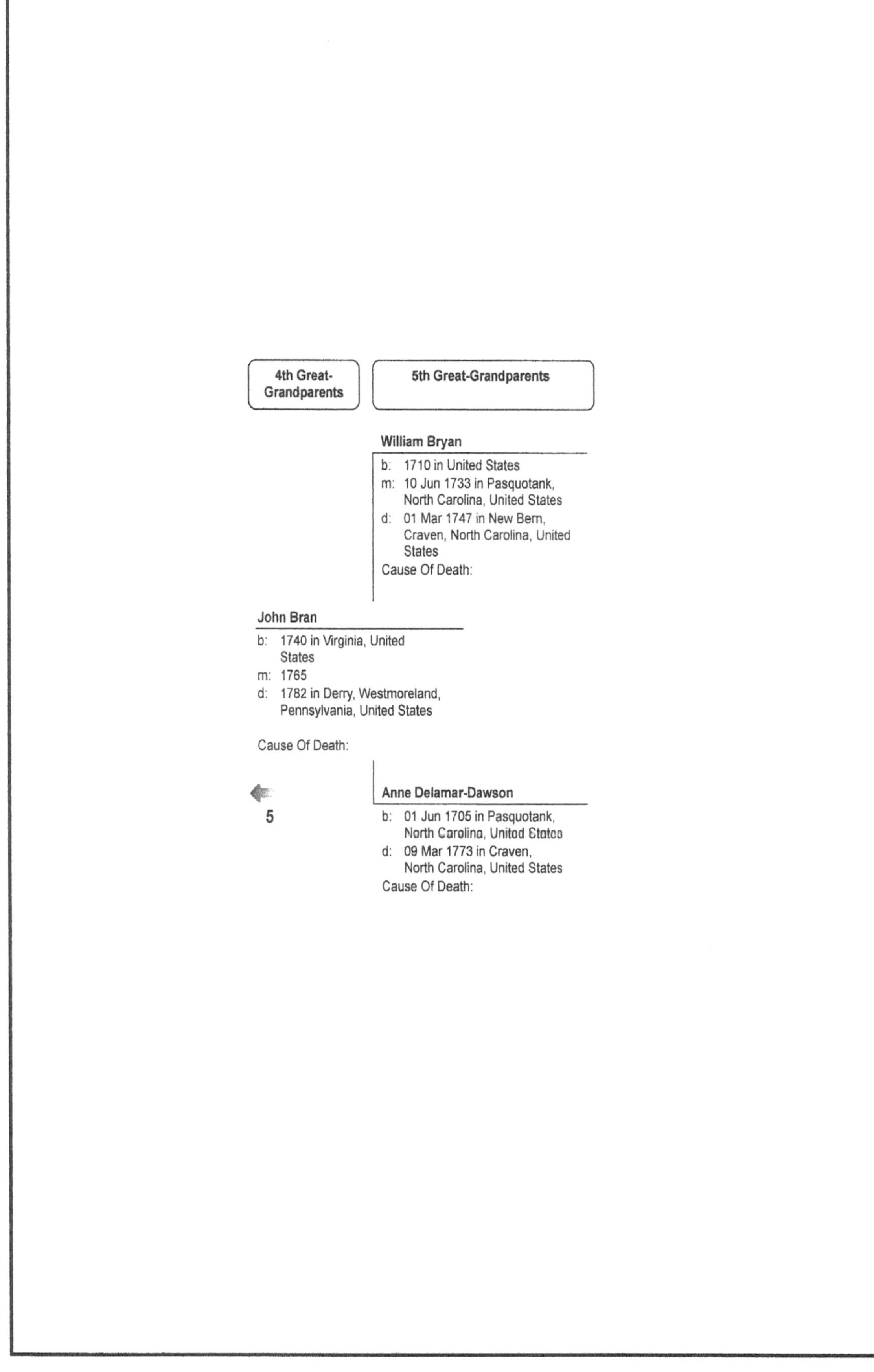

4th Great-Grandparents

5th Great-Grandparents

William Bryan
b: 1710 in United States
m: 10 Jun 1733 in Pasquotank,
      North Carolina, United States
d: 01 Mar 1747 in New Bern,
      Craven, North Carolina, United
      States
Cause Of Death:

John Bran
b: 1740 in Virginia, United
      States
m: 1765
d: 1782 in Derry, Westmoreland,
      Pennsylvania, United States

Cause Of Death:

5

Anne Delamar-Dawson
b: 01 Jun 1705 in Pasquotank,
      North Carolina, United States
d: 09 Mar 1773 in Craven,
      North Carolina, United States
Cause Of Death:

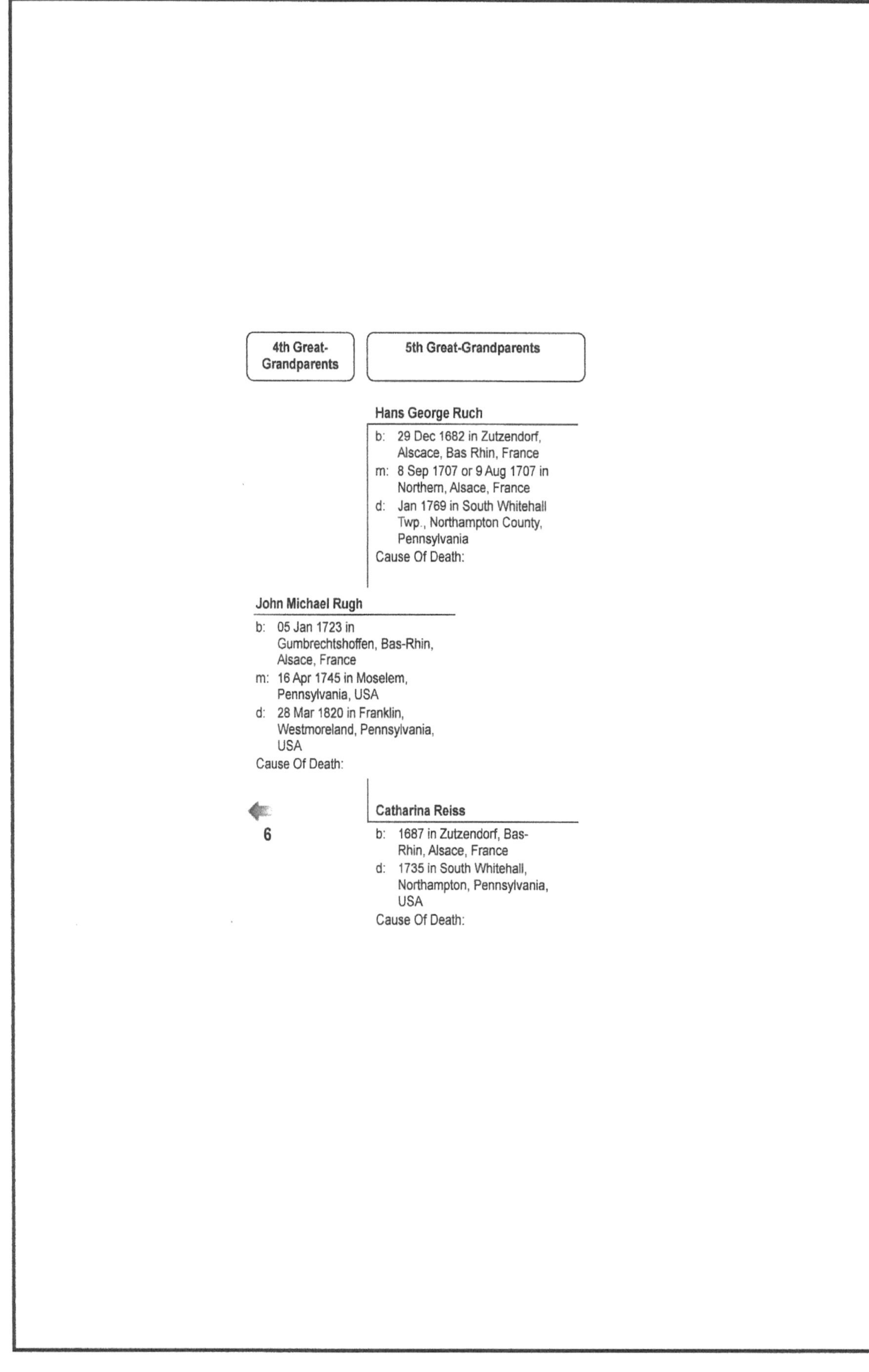

4th Great-Grandparents

5th Great-Grandparents

Hans George Ruch
b: 29 Dec 1682 in Zutzendorf,
    Alscace, Bas Rhin, France
m: 8 Sep 1707 or 9 Aug 1707 in
    Northern, Alsace, France
d: Jan 1769 in South Whitehall
    Twp., Northampton County,
    Pennsylvania
Cause Of Death:

John Michael Rugh
b: 05 Jan 1723 in
    Gumbrechtshoffen, Bas-Rhin,
    Alsace, France
m: 16 Apr 1745 in Moselem,
    Pennsylvania, USA
d: 28 Mar 1820 in Franklin,
    Westmoreland, Pennsylvania,
    USA
Cause Of Death:

6

Catharina Reiss
b: 1687 in Zutzendorf, Bas-
    Rhin, Alsace, France
d: 1735 in South Whitehall,
    Northampton, Pennsylvania,
    USA
Cause Of Death:

<table>
<tr><td>4th Great-Grandparents</td><td>5th Great-Grandparents</td></tr>
</table>

John Christian immigrant Merkel

b: Haßloch, Bad Durkheim, Rheinland-Pfalz, Germany
m: 06 Jan 1707 in Heuchelheim Kirche, Lambsheim, District of Kurpfalz, France

d: 1766 in Moselem Springs, Berks, Pennsylvania, United States
Cause Of Death:

Anna Frantzina Merckling

b: 11 Feb 1717 in Ludwigshafen am Rhein Stadtkreis, Rheinland-Pfalz, Germany
m: 16 Apr 1745 in Moselem, Pennsylvania, USA
d: 13 Jul 1782 in Hannastown, Westmoreland County, Pennsylvania, USA
Cause Of Death:

6

Anna Catharina Bender

b: 02 Dec 1698 in Lambsheim, Ludwigshafen, Rheinland-Pfalz, Germany
d: 11 Apr 1760 in New Hanover, York, Pennsylvania
Cause Of Death:

Andreas Wolffgang Meixel (Meiyssel)

b: @1670 in Austria
m: 17 Mar 1704 in Leimen,
   Baden, Heidelberg, Germany
d: 25 Oct 1739 in Donegal,
   Lancaster, Pennsylvania, USA
Cause Of Death:

Johann Jacob Meixell

b: 14 Jun 1705 in Heidelberg,
   Leimen, Germany
m: 1730 in Conestoga,
   Lancaster, Pennsylvania, USA
d: 18 Jan 1759 in Williams,
   Northampton, PA, USA
Cause Of Death:

7

Anna Maria Schwab

b: 03 Oct 1698 in Sinsheim,
   Rhein-Neckar-Kreis, Baden-
   Württemberg, Germany
d: 09 May 1719 in Leimen,
   Rhein-Neckar-Kreis, Baden-
   Wuerttemberg, Germany
Cause Of Death:

Johannes (John) KITZMILLER

b: bet.1665 and 69 in Waldorf,
Kries Heidelberg, Germany
m: Bef. 1691 in Germany
d: 05 Mar 1747 in Bethel
Township,Lebanon, Pa.
Cause Of Death:

Anna Margaret Maria Kitzmiller

b: 1709 in Leimen, Rhein-
Neckar-Kreis, Baden-
Wuerttemberg, Germany,
m: 1730 in Conestoga,
Lancaster, Pennsylvania, USA
d: 1805 in Leiman, , Baden-
Wuerttemberg, Germany
Cause Of Death:

7

Christina Dyerhin

b: 1670 in Immeldorf, Ansbach,
Bayern, Germany
d: Bef. Aug 1728 in Germany
Cause Of Death:

Do you find reading pedigree charts confusing? Ever wonder why there are arrows on the right side of the page directing you to another page? This chart should help you understand just how many ancestors could be in your pedigree chart...

How many ancestors do you have?

Parents: 2

Grandparents: 4

Great-Grandparents: 8

2nd Great-Grandparents: 16

3rd Great-Grandparents: 32

4th Great-Grandparents: 64

5th Great-Grandparents: 128

6th Great-Grandparents: 256

7th Great-Grandparents: 512

8th Great-Grandparents: 1,024

9th Great-Grandparents: 2,048

10th Great-Grandparents: 4,096

MY BROTHERS
Arthur Rugh – written in 1939

There were five of us Children. After sixty-three years of an unbroken circle both of my brothers died this year of pneumonia.

I suppose they were ordinary men. Certainly we came from ordinary sources. I know of no blue blood in our veins; no crowned heads in our ancestry. My father often said that he never heard of a Rugh who was rich or famous or in jail. Then one of my cousins landed in jail and broke part of that good record.

We grew up on a rocky little farm in Pennsylvania, which much hand work developed into a home which is a very beautiful memory. We went to the village school "after the corn was husked". Our parents were farmers for generations, but both of them for some unknown reason determined that their children should have a higher education. That was not required or always approved in our neighborhood.

We went to one of the three village churches. where loving pastors and pretty farmers' daughters made religion attractive in spite of some archaic theology. We had two sisters who, I thought then and still think, were superb characters.

There was nothing in our inheritance or environment to make my brothers different from the regular variety of men. And yet if all men, or even a minority of men, were like them our world would be a very different world. Ignorance. injustice, poverty and war would not be in the world they worked heroically to build.

C. E. was an educator. H. E. was a lawyer. Both were recognized as first-rate in their profession. There are a good many people who would rise up and call them blessed for the difference that these brothers of mine made in their lives through their profession. But they were much more than successful men in their profession. They were elevated citizens and friends in their communities and loving members of their families. I do not remember a selfish thing either of them ever did. And that is not because the passing years has blurred memory but because they were too absorbed in doing their part of the world's work to be selfish about anything.

Last,spring C. E. took me to a luncheon of one hundred prominent educators of California. The speaker of the day did not arrive. The chairman said "Our speaker is lost but we are not lost. We will turn this meeting over to Charlie Rugh." The torrent of applause was not primarily for a great educator but for a dear friend of them all.

I called with H. E. on an invalid farmer woman. She said "Harry, what is my future when father's pension stops?" Harry said "Forget it." And she knew then, what everybody else in the country knew, that if life's load became too heavy for her "Harry" would carry it. And he did.

My brothers both sang unusually well. C. E. had a lyric first tenor voice. H. E. had a rich full bass voice. They will both be welcomed in Heaven's Choir. They were both good athletes. C. E. was quick as a flash and H. E. was a heady partner or opponent in any game

Both were good farmers. C. E. could plow more ground in a day than the labor law would allow now. And H. E. always plowed the straightest furrow in the township, which was a record to be appreciated. And both liked to argue. Oh, did they! C. E. usually started the argument, and soon discovered he had his hands full. The fun of watching the argument and getting into it, if I could, was that hot as each one fought for his point, you knew they both were interested in something much bigger than winning a debate.

They were both vigorously religious. They travelled from Pennsylvania theological conservatism to a consistent modern position with no loss of any essential and with much vitality of religion. They were charming Christians. Harry's poor health in recent years gave us and many others a good chance to see what a gracious Christian gentleman he always was. He loved his Church. He was an expert Christian whenever any man had needs.

The chief sickness in C.E,'s life was the shock to his nerves when he discovered that when a man was seventy, he was old enough to retire. That was a strange idea to him and with reason. He used his rare pedagogical skill to help many a Bible teacher be a real teacher. Both were elders and pillars in their Churches, patient usually, if not always, with narrow sectarianism.

They both owed much to their homes, our old farm home and their own homes. Both won grand mates and had beautiful children. They both always worked very hard. They would both have lasted, here, past their three score years and ten if they had taken life more easily. But what if they had. It is much happier to remember them working their heads off for somebody for half a century and then leaving us than to think of them saving themselves while somebody needed them.

The processes which made them the grand souls they have been are so simple and so available you wonder why our world is not producing enough men like them to make this the kind of world of which they dreamed and for which they worked so valiantly and so well.

In any case let one "kid brother" record his unmeasurable gratitude for two big brothers who have left no memory which is not an inspiration and who have embodied life as I should like to live it until the sun goes down.

Arthur Rugh was the youngest son of Solomon and Elizabeth Rugh. The four siblings he refers to are Charles E., Harry E., Ida M., and Margaret. Where he connects to your Rugh line is another generation back from Solomon. Solomon was the son of William and Charlotte (Mikesell). His relationship to the Drake girls would then be your 1st Cousin 5x removed.

The Derry Peace Bridge

The Derry Peace Bridge over the River Foyle spans a 400 year old physical and political gap between two sides of a once, bitterly divided community. Designed by Wilkinson Eyre Architects in London and funded to the tune of £14 million by the European Regional Development Fund for Peace, it is a very impressive and elegant piece of architecture. With two structural arms heading in opposite directions, symbolizing the unification of both communities from the opposite sides of the Foyle river, the Protestant Waterside and the Nationalist Bogside, these two opposed and independent arms are now united in a symbolic handshake across the river. Opened in 2011, this 235 metre long, 4 metre wide curved footpath, track and cycleway stretches from the Guild Hall in the city centre of Derry City to Ebrington Square and St Columb's Park on the far side of the River Foyle.

The Derry Peace Bridge has become an integral part of Derry City's infrastructure and has changed the way local people use and view their city, with over 3 million people having crossed it so far and many of the locals using it daily. Popular 24/7 it is never empty and while it certainly tells the local story of triumph over adversity it is nonetheless a universal symbol of peace that locals and visitors alike can relate to and resonate with. The bridge was deliberately constructed with a significant curve from end to end. The message is that the "Road to peace is never a straight line."

I am very Proud
of
My Scots Irish Roots
An Irish Sense of Humor

Do you know the old Scottish legend
of how the thistle came to be
the flower of Scotland?

The story goes that an invading Norse army
planned to ambush the Scots
by slaughtering them while they slept.
This attack required as much stealth as possible
so the invaders attacked barefoot.
Unfortunately for them, one of the attackers
stepped on a thistle,
and his cries of pain were enough
to wake the sleeping Scotsmen,
who charged into battle
and defeated their enemies.

And so the thistle was named
The Flower of Scotland

Marti Bennett is a retired Jr.-Sr. High health and physical ed teacher from Titusville, PA, Marti first became interested in genetic health when her mother was diagnosed with Parkinson's. The family health research quickly turned into a hobby, with a greater appreciation for history. Inspired by the TV series "Who Do You Think You Are?," Marti's research branched out to include historical events. Fortunately, there are a multitude of Internet sites for amateur genealogists, plus the long Pennsylvania winters offer ample time for research.

www.ingramcontent.com/pod-product-compliance
Lightning Source LLC
Chambersburg PA
CBHW040140240726
48664CB00002B/550